Real Life MATH MYSTERIES

Real Life MATH MYSTERIES

A KIDS' ANSWER TO THE QUESTION, "WHAT WILL WE EVER USE THIS FOR?"

MARY FORD WASHINGTON

ISBN-10: 1-882664-14-0
ISBN-13: 978-1-882664-14-6

Prufrock Press Inc.
P.O. Box 8813
Waco, TX 76714-8813
(800) 998-2208
Fax: (800) 240-0333
http://www.prufrock.com

dedicated to my children

Carmen, Carrie, Esther, and David

Special thanks to my students
Sierra, Ben, Scott, and John
for their assistance with this project.

Special thanks also
to the wonderful people of Marshfield, Wisconsin,
who freely gave their time, encouragement, and assistance
to provide this look into the real world of math.

Contents

About Real Life Math Mysteries

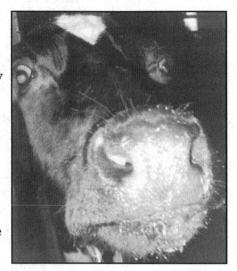

All of the problems in this book were created by individuals in the author's hometown of Marshfield, WI. The problems came from each person's day-to-day experiences within their careers. Marshfield is located in central Wisconsin. It has 20,000 people more or less, and almost as many cows. There are also lots of ducks and geese, pickup trucks, dress shops, bars, farmers, toads, turtles, deerhunters, rabbits, doctors, snowmobiles, wildflowers, deer, butterflies, bicycles, factory workers, mosquitoes, and lawn ornaments.

The people on the following pages are real people and so are the math problems they describe.

+ - x √ π ± ÷ ≥ + - x √ π ± ÷ ≥

Abbreviations and Symbols You'll Need to Know

#	pound
lb	pound
oz	ounce
"	inch
'	foot
yd	yard
mi	mile
ml	milliliter
%	percent
#	number
F	Fahrenheit
°	degrees
/	per (as in gallons/minute)
x	by (as in 12' x 16')
d	diameter
r	radius
c	circumference
π	pi (3.1417)

Note to Teachers

Like you, probably, I didn't always love math. While I was growing up, math seemed more like a set of rituals than a way to think logically.

Like you, probably, as a teacher I applauded the new math standards outlined by the National Council of Teachers of Mathematics, but found them difficult to wholly institute in the artificial world of my rectangular classroom. Though preferable to isolated drill and practice, even the "enlightened" math materials I could find seemed lacking in reality. It is easy to agree that students need to be able to visualize math concepts in a real world setting, but how that should be done is another matter.

My hope, then, in the formation of this book is to add to the sparse body of relevant and exciting NCTM-type math materials for students. Many hours were spent collecting real-life math problems from the lives of professional people in our little city. The response from the community was enthusiastic and helpful. A horse breeder, a police detective, a lawyer, a newspaper editor, the mayor, an airplane pilot, a dairy farmer, a veterinarian, a truck driver, and a fast-food restaurant manager are among those who contributed to this book. It doesn't get any more real-life than this.

My recommendation is that you don't stop with *Real Life Math Mysteries*. I encourage you to contact people in your own community and develop a math program based on your own neighbors' daily math application … a curriculum which your students will be able to visualize … real world math.

The possibilities are endless. And attainable.

Real Life Math Mysteries and the NCTM Standards

This book has been designed to conform to the National Council of Teachers of Mathematics goals, as outlined in *The*

NCTM Curriculum and Evaluation Standards for School Mathematics.

✔ By assisting students to visualize the settings of math problems and guaranteeing their actuality in a real world setting, students are **encouraged to value mathematics** as relevant and vital in their own communities.

✔ It is expected that using this book will **enhance students' confidence in their abilities** by providing significant challenges which allow for a sense of accomplishment when achieved, and further, offer the student who accomplishes them a realistic step in the realization of career preparedness for the future.

✔ Certainly this book allows for the student to become a **mathematical problem solver**. There are no easy answers here; no single formula or repetition makes for robot-like answer-finding. Rather, common sense is the only way out of each question posed, and because each problem is so different, each requires the full participation of the learner with ample expenditure of thought and effort.

✔ **Communication** is key to these problems. Students must acquire from the written descriptions of each of these unique problems the understanding to derive answers. In other cases, such as the one offered by Mayor Daniels, the answer is already clear—the students' task is then to present the knowledge in its most effective graphic form. The use of technology is promoted through the teaching of advanced calculator skills and computer graphing.

✔ Of first importance, *Real Life Math Mysteries* was developed to assist students to **grow in mathematical reasoning skills**. The real situations provide for students a conceptual setting upon which to build and expand their thinking and reasoning, somewhat like installing an arbor for a grape vine.

Without going into further detail, let it be said that *Real Life Math Mysteries* provides the connections between a child's real world, the academic world, and the adult world of work. In fact, it would be hard to find a book more closely in line with the National Council of Teachers of Mathematics directives.

Important Note

Very few of these problems are easy. Some require the students to struggle.

Unless the students are highly motivated and gifted mathematically, they will appreciate some guidance from time to time as they puzzle through these problems. In some classes it will be preferable to work together as a whole, but the teacher should resist the temptation to make these problems too easy by giving too much assistance.

You may wish to ban the use of calculators for these problems, but I have not. The book was designed with the use of calculators in mind, except those problems which are otherwise indicated.

Also, please note the methods for solutions provided in this answer key are simply one version. Students who are able to derive the solution in different ways should be encouraged to do so. Class discussion can determine which method is most efficient.

It is also important to note that, because these problems are from real life, answers can vary slightly due to rounding. There are many choices as to when to round and to what degree. Any answer which can be justified by the student using logical mathematical reasoning should be accepted.

Your comments and suggestions are welcomed. Please direct correspondence to:

Mary Ford Washington
Washington School
Marshfield, Wisconsin 54449
or phone (715) 387-1238.

I hope you enjoy using the book as much as I have enjoyed creating it.

+ - x √ π ± ÷ ≥ + - x √ π ± ÷ ≥

Real Life Math Problems

+ - x √ π ± ÷ ≥ + - x √ π ± ÷ ≥

Associated Bank

Marty Reinhart is the vice president of Associated Bank, so, of course, he uses math all the time.

Interestingly, Mr. Reinhart says math was not one of his favorite subjects. "I remember in ninth grade the teacher called me up to the chalkboard because he said I was the one who needed the most help. Later, I had a teacher who helped me earn straight As, and math became my favorite subject.

"I'm not sure I remember all the algebraic equations I learned, or all of my geometry. But math taught me a way to think, and that has carried over to all areas of my life. You see, math is being able to look at a complex situation, organize it in your mind, analyze it, and then develop a solution for it. And that's not any different from what you have to do in life."

$+ - \times \sqrt{} \pi \pm \div \geq + - \times \sqrt{} \pi \pm \div \geq$

$+ - \times \sqrt{} \pi \pm \div \geq + - \times \sqrt{} \pi \pm \div \geq + - \times \sqrt{} \pi \pm \div \geq + - \times \sqrt{} \pi \pm \div \geq + - \times \sqrt{} \pi \pm$

2   *Real Life Math Mysteries*

Here are some problems I encounter on a daily basis:

- The first problem concerns saving money. Suppose I worked hard and saved $1,000 per year for 10 years. I earned an interest rate of 8% per year (figured annually).

   What would I earn in interest over the entire 10-year period?

> ### Problem Solving Strategy: Make A Chart
>
> **Remember, interest will be calculated 10 times over the 10-year period, and each year, he is adding $1,000. A chart can help you keep track of all those changes.**

- The second problem concerns borrowing money. Suppose I wanted to buy a motorcycle. I borrowed $5,000 from the bank today and agreed to make monthly payments of $161.34 for three years.

   How much interest will I have paid at the end of the three years?

Mike Kupfer enjoys his job at Schalow's Nursery. He must—he has worked there since he was 14 years old. Mr. Kupfer started working for Schalow's as a weed-puller, then went on to earn a college degree in horticulture and landscape design. Now he supervises all of the landscape crews, and that means lots of math for Mr. Kupfer.

+ - x √ π ± ÷ ≥ + - x √ π ± ÷ ≥

• A family has asked us to put in a 12 x 16 foot brick patio behind their house. Brick comes bundled together in a pallet, which we take apart when we get to the job.

Knowing that there are 89 square feet of brick in a pallet, how many pallets will I need to order?

• When we're laying out a patio, the first thing we have to do is make sure the lines we use to outline it are square to the house. For that, we use the formula discovered by Pythagorus a long time ago which says that in a right angle, the sum of the sides squared will equal the diagonal squared. The formula looks like this: $a^2 + b^2 = c^2$.

Now we have measured out 12 feet from the house, and we have measured 16 feet along the house.

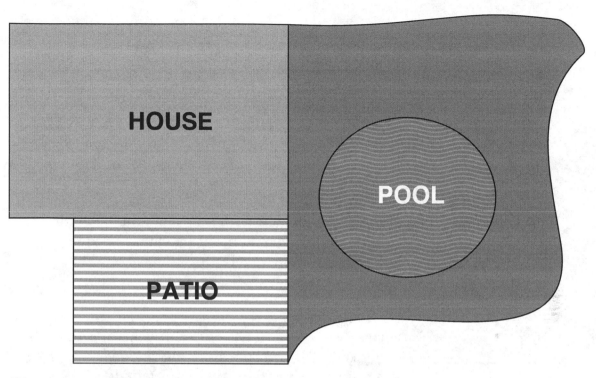

How can we find out if the patio borders we have drawn are square with the house?

- **Roses will be placed every 3 feet around the circumference of the 18' diameter pool. Each will be planted 1¹/₂' from the edge. How many roses will we plant? (Hint: c = π x d)**

"I always liked math, and that's good because most of the math we have to do we do in our heads. We especially use math in designing and estimating, where there's a lot of geometry. When I was in school I often thought, 'Why am I learning this?' Now I know why. I use it every day."

ROGER E. KROGSTAD, D.V.M.

(715) 387-1225

Wildwood Animal Hospital

217 W. 14th St. ● MARSHFIELD, WI 54449

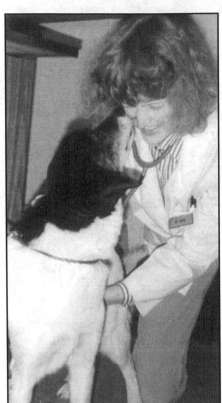

Elizabeth Knabe, DVM

Dr. Elizabeth Knabe says she likes her job as a veterinarian with Wildwood Animal Hospital.

"I didn't start out with a love of math. I think I probably thought I would never use math in my later life. … But now—we're always using math, and I consider the calculator my friend.

"Nobody should be scared by mathematics. It's something everyone needs. When I went to college only 40 percent of the people studying to be vets were female. Now more than 60 percent are female.

"Here's an example from my job."

+ - x √ π ± ÷ ≥ + - x √ π ± ÷ ≥

I have a young collie with a virus. It's having vomiting and diarrhea and is getting dehydrated. I need to start an intravenous (in the vein) fluid drip so that it won't get dehydrated.

The collie will need 1,920 ml/day. The fluid drip chamber delivers fluids in drops, and 15 drops = 1 ml.

How often should I set the drip chamber to drip in order to deliver the total (1,920 ml) in 24 hours?

MARSHFIELD

HEART
CARE

1000 NORTH OAK AVENUE
MARSHFIELD, WI 54449

1-800-888-4755

FAX
715-389-4555

Ron Menaker

"I flunked algebra. At the time I didn't appreciate it. In fact, I didn't appreciate the value of an education. Now I have an advanced degree in finance, and I am a certified public accountant (CPA)."

Ron Menaker is also assistant director of operations for the Marshfield Clinic, one of the largest rural health care facilities in the nation. Mr. Menaker uses lots of math in his position, and he enjoys it.

"The thing I like about math is the discipline. It's the structure of my life. To me, math is the order ... the facts ... the left brain ... the logic ... the should-be's. It's the rational foundation for any decision making.

"There is a mathematical formula that we can use to look at many of the issues that arise here at the clinic. In order to judge the value of any new idea, physicians and administrators have to look at what it would mean in terms of improvement of services to our patients, and then divide that figure by the cost.

"Another way to look at it is—value equals effectiveness over efficiency. Through this process we arrive at what we hope is a reasonable decision."

Here's an example of one of the decisions Mr. Menaker makes at the clinic.

+ - x √ π ± ÷ ≥ + - x √ π ± ÷ ≥

I am an administrator for the cardiology department. Many of its patients are very sick. This department has 15 cardiologists (doctors who work with the heart). We are being asked frequently if we can provide more services to other clinics in northern Wisconsin. The question we have to answer is whether we have enough time to help out other clinics.

Each of the 15 cardiologists can see approximately 10 patients per day Monday through Friday. In a 365-day year, each cardiologist is off on weekends, and has 25 vacation days, 12 educational/meeting days, and 14 other business and scientific-related days when he or she is not available to see patients.

- **Do we have enough cardiologists to see the 30,000 patients we expect to see in Marshfield in the next year *and* have time to help out these other clinics in northern Wisconsin?**

- **If so, and this available time is divided equally among the staff, how many days would each doctor be available to assist other clinics?**

+ - x √ π ± ÷ ≥ + - x √ π ± ÷ ≥

"The trick in my job is to take the creative, the imaginative, and the reality of the way things are and to integrate them with the math, the system, and the logic of the way things should be, in order to make patient care better. ... Math for me is the foundation for rationally improving life."

Ellie Brubacker

Ellie Brubacker is the manager of Pizza Hut in Marshfield. Does she use much math? You bet!

"Does anybody like math when they're in school? That was probably one of my least favorite subjects. But it sure helps now.

"I would be totally lost without knowing math. From figuring prices, coupons, getting averages, using the calculator, to ordering, even keeping track of cleaning supplies … I could never figure this stuff out if I didn't know math."

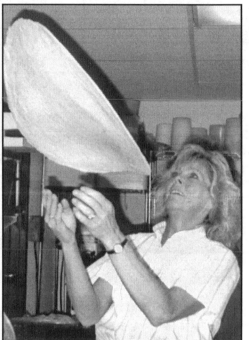

+ - x √ π ± ÷ ≥ + - x √ π ± ÷ ≥

- In order to know how much of any supply to buy from week to week, I really have to keep track of what we use. For example, lettuce—I keep a running account of how much we use each day.

What's the minimum amount of lettuce I should order for next week?

<u>Last Week's Lettuce Use</u>

	Head lettuce	Romaine lettuce
Sunday	$2^3/4$ head lettuce,	$1^1/2$ Romaine lettuce
Monday	$1^3/4$ head lettuce,	$1/2$ Romaine lettuce
Tuesday	$1^1/4$ head lettuce,	$1/4$ Romaine lettuce
Wednesday	$1^1/2$ head lettuce,	1 Romaine lettuce
Thursday	$1^1/2$ head lettuce,	$1/2$ Romaine lettuce
Friday	$3^1/2$ head lettuce,	2 Romaine lettuce
Saturday	$3^1/4$ head lettuce,	$1^1/4$ Romaine lettuce

"In actual fact, it's hard to tell how much of any item we are going to use. Sometimes I run out, sometimes I order way too much. But keeping track of statistics like this really helps."

- The measuring of toppings seems simple enough, but that is one area that can get kind of confusing for new workers here. We have different color cups for different measures. For example, the recipe for one of our pizzas calls for one red cup of pepperoni, a green cup of mushrooms, and a blue cup of cheese.

  If a customer asks for the pizza to be half pepperoni/cheese/mushroom and the other half double cheese/mushroom, how much or how many of what cups of each color do we use?

- Here's a question for you. One bag of dough can be tossed into 23 small pizzas, 13 medium pizzas, or 8 large pizzas. Dough comes 4 bags to a bundle, and I always order a couple extra bundles. Our computer keeps a running total of how much we sell each day.

  From what you see of last week's pizza sales, how many bundles of dough should I order to cover next week's hand-tossed pizzas?

  <u>LAST WEEK'S DAILY SALES: HAND-TOSSED PIZZAS</u>

	THURS	FRI	SAT	SUN	MON	TUES	WED
SMALL	16	18	18	18	16	16	16
MEDIUM	24	29	29	29	24	24	24
LARGE	20	23	23	23	20	20	19

JUNEAU
MINDER
GROSS &
STEVNING-ROE, S.C.

Attorneys-at-Law

Ann Stevning-Roe is the mother of two, a cross-country skier, an avid biker, and an attorney at the law firm Juneau, Minder, Gross & Stevning-Roe, S.C.

"Greetings! As an attorney, I use math every day. When one party owes another money, it is common for them to come to me for legal advice. Sometimes I represent the business or person to whom the money is owed.

"Here is the type of problem I often face."

+ - x √ π ± ÷ ≥ + - x √ π ± ÷ ≥

- A judgment in the amount of $20,000 was entered on October 8. The rate of interest is 12% per annum (per year).

  Calculate what the payoff will be on the judgment if it is paid on December 20 of the same year.

  The following costs also need to be added:
  - abstractor fees for continuation of the abstract $130;
  - filing fee $78;
  - service fee $36;
  - postage $27; and
  - photocopies $33.

  What will be the amount needed for the final payoff?

First you must figure the amount of interest which must be paid:

Interest =
percentage of interest x total judgment x percentage of a year

> **Problem Solving Strategy: Write an Equation**
>
> Writing an equation can help you think a problem through.

THE LUCAS FARM

Victor and Sally Lucas own 337 acres just south of the city, where they grow corn, hay, oats, and soybeans, and raise 145 head of Holsteins and beef cattle.

"There is just an incredible amount of math in farming. Some people think that we just throw the seed in the ground and it will grow. That is a total misconception.

"As a farmer, you have to know how to plant to get the highest production per acre, you have to know the pH of your soil, you have to know your planting array, and your germination rate, your silo's storage capacity, and the moisture content of your crop. You have to know which herbicides to use and how much per acre. And that's just the beginning."

+ - x √ π ± ÷ ≥ + - x √ π ± ÷ ≥

- I plant several varieties of seed, and I get information about the seed from the labels. The label on one 50# bag of soybeans says there are 2,700 seeds per pound in the bag. Another one says it has 2,592 seeds per pound. So I roughly average the two. I want to plant 250,000 seeds per acre.

  How many bags will I need to plant 10 acres?

- I can only expect 92% of the seeds to germinate.

  How many plants can I expect to grow on 10 acres?

- Figuring milk production is more math. I have a 415-gallon tank, and I know that a gallon of milk weighs 8.5 pounds. On average my cows are producing 55 pounds of milk a day.

  What is the maximum herd I can keep with a daily milk pick-up?

- We vary a cow's feed by how much milk it gives.

A cow giving 80# a day needs:

grain mix	27.1 pounds/day
hay	20.0 pounds
corn silage	25.0 pounds
protein, etc.	4.0 pounds

A cow giving 100# a day needs:

grain mix	25.7 pounds
hay	20.0 pounds
corn silage	31.2 pounds
protein, etc.	8.3 pounds

Figure how many pounds of feed a cow giving 70 pounds of milk needs.

Problem Solving Strategy: Make A Table

Organizing the information into a table can help you think more clearly about it. Make a table showing grain, hay, corn, and protein requirements for a cow giving 70, 80, 90, and 100 pounds of milk a day. First fill in the information you know; then find the new data.

+ - x √ π ± ÷ ≥ + - x √ π ± ÷ ≥

"And then we have to figure profit, and we have to figure that quite closely. In most businesses it is considered essential to have 15% profit to stay in operation. Farmers operate below that, more like 7%-10%, and we still function. It's been calculated that a farmer's average pay is about 85 cents an hour. Our average day is 14 hours. Twenty-hour days are common.

"I enjoyed math in school, and I took algebra, geometry, trigonometry, and college chemistry and calculus. Work hard in math. Everything you do you need math for. No matter what job you end up with, you still have to balance your checkbook and you still have to know percent and interest if you plan on buying anything.

"Math? I use it every day, every cotton-picking day."

SIDE KIX
TAEKWON-DO

Glen A. Beaudry

"EEACH! BLENCH! NEEEONAH!"

Black Belt Glen Beaudry is instructing his class in the art of Taekwon-do, and believe it or not, it involves plenty of math. Mr. Beaudry's students have to understand angles in order to achieve proper body position.

A precise block is achieved only if the elbow bends at a 90° angle and the arm is positioned at a 45° angle from the body. Kicks also must be positioned exactly—0° is used to describe straight ahead, 90° to the right, 180° straight back.

Speed is a key element in Taekwon-do, because the faster you are, the more powerful your moves. Speed is measured in terms of velocity, or feet per second.

To find the velocity of a punch or kick, Mr. Beaudry uses this formula:

Velocity = distance (feet) / **time (seconds)**

which is the same as:

Velocity = distance ÷ speed

When you know the *velocity* of the movement (how fast it traveled in feet per second), as well as the weight behind it (*mass*), you can find the *power* of the movement in foot pounds.

$$P = \frac{1}{2}(m)(v^2)$$

To find out how much power is behind their punch, students in Mr. Beaudry's class stand 30 inches from an electronic target.

The device flashes a pulsing red light and measures the time until the students' punch. Normal reaction time, which is the time it takes a student to notice the light and to begin moving, is 0.2 seconds, and is subtracted from the measurement.

+ - x √ π ± ÷ ≥ + - x √ π ± ÷ ≥

- A student who weighs 145 pounds was timed by the device at 0.4 seconds.

  Can you calculate how many foot pounds of force were behind his punch?

Problem Solving Strategy: Write Down Each Step

Writing down each step may sound like a lot of work, but if you don't, your head could be swimming by the end of this problem. Mathematicians always record each step of their calculations for three reasons:
- So they can keep track of the parts of a complex problem;
- So they can recheck their work to find errors; and
- So they can explain their solutions to someone else.

Use a calculator. Mr. Beaudry does.

FOREIGN AUTOMOTIVE SERVICE

10519 Hwy A
Marshfield, WI 54449

715-387-4500

Mike W. Manicke
Donna M. Manicke

Donna and Mike Manicke have run
Foreign Automotive Service for years.
Mike manages the mechanical aspect,
and Donna handles the appointments,
scheduling, and ordering.

Running a business is complicated, and
fixing cars has never been harder. Mike
says, "With the complexity of today's cars, mechanics have to
have the kind of intelligence and the knowledge base that
someone like a doctor would have to have."

+ - x √ π ± ÷ ≥ + - x √ π ± ÷ ≥

We have three mechanics and only two hoists. We work from 8
a.m. until 5 p.m. with an hour for lunch. Assuming that one out
of every seven appointments that I schedule will call at the last
minute to cancel, how many of the jobs listed below should I
schedule for tomorrow?

And there are a few other things to consider:

Donna: "Be sure to leave a few gaps in the schedule for the
   unexpected."
Mike: "Like when we look under the hood, we might find something else wrong."
Donna: "Or sometimes the supplier sends the wrong part."

Mike: "There are all kinds of equation-changers we deal with every day around here."

Donna: "We talk to ourselves a lot in this business."

SCHEDULE

1) 1984 Nissan 200SX Turbo
   Replace head gasket.
   This will be an 8-hour job, figuring it will have to be on the hoist half the time.

2) 1985 Audi 5000
   Replace the engine.
   This is an 8 hour job, half the job requires hoist.

3) 1991 Honda Civic Wagon
   Check brakes, 45 minutes.
   Investigate rattle, 15 minutes.
   Requires hoist for both.

4) 1988 Nissan 200 SX
   Replace muffler pipe.
   Normally 30 minutes on the hoist, but car is rusty, might take longer.

5) 1990 Mercedes
   Replace idler arm, check rear end noise.
   One hour, hoist not needed.

6) 1991 Golf
   Replace CV boot.
   1.5 hour on hoist.

Problem Solving Strategy: Make A Chart

Make a chart showing the two hoists, the three mechanics, and the hourly schedule. Now try to fill in the schedule.

$+ - x \sqrt{} \pi \pm \div \geq + - x \sqrt{} \pi \pm \div \geq + - x \sqrt{} \pi \pm \div \geq + - x \sqrt{} \pi \pm \div \geq + - x \sqrt{} \pi \pm$

Real Life Math Mysteries   17

MARATHON TRAVEL SHOPS
an NCI Company

"Since 1949"

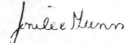

Jonilee Gunn enjoys her job as a travel agent with Marathon Travel in Marshfield.

Here is a typical problem she is faced with.

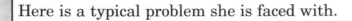

+ - x √ π ± ÷ ≥ + - x √ π ± ÷ ≥

A gentleman representing a group of 36 people just came to Marathon Travel hoping to sign up for a 25-day escorted tour of Australia, New Zealand, and the South Pacific. The group will fly from Los Angeles to Tahiti. There they will tour the islands via boat, observing Polynesian music and dancing amid the lush native foliage. Next they will cruise by catamaran to the Great Barrier Reef to snorkel amid the brightly-colored corals and fish. A Jeep tour of the Australian outback and a visit with Aborigines will conclude with a camel ride through the bush. Another day, they will embark on a flightseeing tour over the snow-capped peaks, glaciers, and sheep ranches. Further adventures will take them to visit a Maori village and a bubbling hot spring.

How much will this adventure cost?

- A group tour of this type might have an initial cost per person of $2,779. Our travel agency booking fees will add 11% more to the initial cost (rounded to the nearest dollar), and international taxes will add another $36. However, for larger groups, special discounts are often offered by the tour company. This particular tour provides that for every 30 people booked, one more person may travel entirely free. The gentleman told me that the group had decided to split up the extra savings among them.

What will the price be for each person going on this tour?

ROEHL
Transport Inc.

Mark G. Hostetter

Mark Hostetter is a truck driver for Roehl Transport Inc., and in order to keep in compliance with Department of Transportation government safety regulations, Mr. Hostetter has to keep track of a lot of math.

After a good night's sleep, Mr. Hostetter is awakened at 7:30 a.m. on April 1st by a call from his dispatcher.

His dispatcher has a load for him to take to Porter, IN, right away. Porter is 510 miles away. He plans as if the trip were 10% longer because of detours, traffic jams, and the like.

Roehl truck drivers average 50 miles per hour.

- U.S. Department of Transportation regulations prohibit a driver from driving more than 70 hours in an 8-day period. Over the past 7 days, Mr. Hostetter has accumulated 54³/4 hours.

Knowing this, does he have enough hours available to deliver the freight today?

- At 8 p.m., Mr. Hostetter's log looks like this.

  DOT regulations state that no driver shall drive more than 10 hours without following it with eight consecutive hours off duty.

DRIVER'S DAILY LOG April 1st	
Midnight - 8 a.m.	off duty
8 a.m. - 8:15 a.m.	truck inspection
8:15 a.m. - 1 p.m.	driving
1 p.m. - 1:30 p.m.	off duty
1:30 p.m. - 6:30 p.m.	driving
6:30 p.m. - 6:45 p.m.	truck inspection/report
6:45 p.m. - 8 p.m.	off duty
8 p.m. -	driving

To the nearest quarter hour, what is the earliest he will arrive in Porter? (deduct 15 minutes for another truck inspection after his rest.)

Widmare
STABLES

Carol Willmert - Weigel

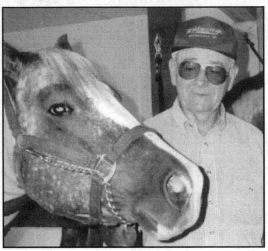

Jake Weigel and his wife Carol own and operate Widmare Stables in Marshfield. To give you an idea of the size of the operation, **mentally calculate the cost of the two miles of white fencing installed in 1989.** The fence cost $7.50 a foot, and there are more than 5,000 feet in a mile. That is just a sample of the math involved in running this huge operation.

The Weigels are preparing to take five of their horses to international competition, where they expect at least some of the horses to place in the top 10. Proper diet is essential to raising champion horses, and each one has a specified feed mixture. Individualizing each horse's diet can make ordering feed a complicated undertaking.

- **According to the feeding schedule on the next page, how many bales of hay the Weigels should expect to order in an average 30-day month?**

- **How long should they expect a ton of grain to last?**

Widmare Stables Feeding Schedule
(The horses are fed the prescribed amounts
twice a day unless otherwise indicated.)

Horse's Name	Description	Grain*	Hay†
Audra	Shetland Pony	1 handful	2 slices
Zanny	Yearling	3/4 can	2 slices
Sis	Quarter Horse	1 can	1 slice
Memphis	Pony of America	3/4 can	2 slices
Expo	Quarter Horse	3/4 can	2 slices
Might Cut Up	Appaloosa Stallion	1 can	3 slices
Chip N' Zee	P.O.A. Stallion (pictured with Jake)	1½ cans	2 slices
Max	Arabian	½ can	2 slices
Skye	Appaloosa Gelding	½ can	2 slices
Baron	Arabian	3/4 can	2 slices
Classy Chasi	Appaloosa	1 can	2 slices
Dixie	P.O.A. Mare	1 can	2 slices
Triples	Appaloosa Mare	1 can	2 slices
Zip Dude	Quarter Horse Colt	1 can	2 slices
Fired Up	Appaloosa Colt	1 can	2 slices
Cash	P.O.A. Colt	½ can	2 slices
DeeDee	Appaloosa	none	3 slices
Alicia	Appaloosa	½ can	2 slices
Lori	P.O.A. Mare	1¼ can	2 slices
Rose	Foxtrotter	none	3 slices
Cuhotka	Appaloosa	½ can	2 slices
Marty	Appaloosa Gelding	½ can	2 slices
Gitty	Thoroughbred	¼ can	3 slices
Seamis	Thoroughbred	½ can	3 slices
Leggs	Quarterhorse Gelding	3/4 can	2 slices
Farchild	Holsteiner	½ can	3 slices
Hey There	Appaloosa	¼ can	3 slices
Charlie	Morgan/Shetland	¼ a.m. only	1 slice
Other Yearlings		none	2 bales
Other Mares With Foals		1½ cans	2 bales

The rest of the horses are out to pasture.

*   Four pounds of grain will fill one coffee can.

†   There are 12 slices of hay in a bale.

THE BOSON COMPANY INC.
CONTRACTORS
MANAGERS
DEVELOPERS

As chief architectural estimator for the Boson Company, Ron Patterson is responsible for determining the cost of building a building before one brick is ever laid, before one piling is in place, and before the ground is even cleared.

"Precision is key to the contracting business," says Mr. Patterson. "If we estimate our costs too high, another contractor will put in a lower bid and get the job. However, if we estimate our costs too low, we'll be in big trouble later on.

"The job of constructing businesses and schools entails many complexities which become further challenges to the estimator. Finding the cubic volume of four walls 9" wide and 4' 0" in height isn't difficult, but remember that the builder will not need to use as much concrete at the corners as the outside measurements may seem to indicate. This is called the 'takeoff,' and in a large building with many corners, if the takeoff is not accurate, the cumulative error will be significant."

+ - x √ π ± ÷ ≥ + - x √ π ± ÷ ≥

Let's say our job for today is to **calculate the number of cubic**

Problem Solving Strategy: Write a Word Equation

You know that volume = length x width x height (or depth). This problem is only a little more complicated than that. Keep in mind what you are finding, and write each step neatly so you don't lose track of what you are finding.

yards of Redi-mix concrete needed to pour the foundation walls and floor for a 24'0" x 24'0" garage. The foundation wall is to be 4'0" tall and 9" wide. The floor inside the four walls is to be 6" thick. Concrete is only sold by the full cubic yard. Here's a hint: it is easier to convert the inches to feet (in decimals) before you begin. The rest is up to you.

P.S. This is one of those problems where you will be thankful for the calculator.

outside wall measurement 24' 0"

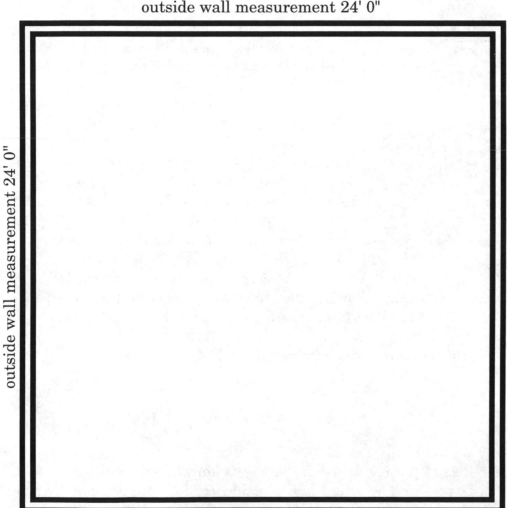

Foundation plan
Overhead view

MARSHFIELD
The City in the Center
POLICE DEPARTMENT

Detective Jepsen has been with the Marshfield Police Force for 12 years. "Math is extremely important in law enforcement. For example, the calculations for lie detector and polygraph exams are all mathematical … to become certified to give alcohol testing you have to understand and be able to use decimals … in order to get radar certification you better know your math … to figure shifts and the rotation of schedules, you need to be able to calculate and use formulas, or you're going to be lost … the list goes on and on.

"I like working with numbers, and for that reason I am frequently assigned investigations related to money crimes. Those crimes would include arson for profit, embezzlement, forgery, and major thefts. When I conduct these types of investigations, I try to find out as much as I can about a suspect's money matters. This might include any insurance settlements paid out and bank account records.

"Here's an example of a case I might be assigned."

+ - x √ π ± ÷ ≥ + - x √ π ± ÷ ≥

Recently, a residence in the city of Marshfield was discovered to be on fire. The owner of the residence, John Smith, could not be located for two days. It was found that he was out of town visiting his mother in Stevens Point, 35 miles away. I was called to the fire scene and soon conducted a "cause and origin" investigation. Three points of origin were located for the fire, and there did not appear to be a legitimate cause at any point.

Samples of ash were taken at each point and a liquid accelerant (gasoline) was detected in each of the samples.

This type of information would offer enough evidence that the fire was purposefully set, and we could state it was arson. We must now prove who was responsible for the setting of the fire and the motive for setting it.

John Smith bought this home in 1989. He has tried to sell the house for the past four years. Some of the neighbors who have been interviewed state that he hates living in Wisconsin and wants to move south but cannot afford it. Smith's mother was contacted and stated that her son arrived at her house about 10 minutes before the fire was discovered.

All of these facts indicate that Mr. Smith should be considered a good suspect. A subpoena is obtained through the courts allowing me to obtain all of Mr. Smith's financial records. The following is the result of this records search:
    Mr. Smith makes $1,250 per month.
    Mr. Smith currently owes $54,012.90 for his home;
    His monthly payment is $686.40.
    He also pays $2,400 per year in real estate taxes.

He used to pay $180 per year in insurance for his house, but he recently changed his insurance and now pays $240 per year. This change in insurance occurred on March 1, 1993, and increased the payoff on his home from $70,000 to $100,000.

Further monthly obligations:
    Car payments, $250.
    Master Card, $30.
    Household Finance, $40.
    State Bank, boat payment, $120.
    Utilities (gas, electricity, phone) $105.

- **Can you show that Mr. Smith may have had a motive for setting this fire?**

Incidentally, Mr. Smith removed his boat before the fire and took it to his mother's house. (Hint: There is still ice on the lakes in March.)

WDLB • AM
GOETZ BROADCASTING CORPORATION

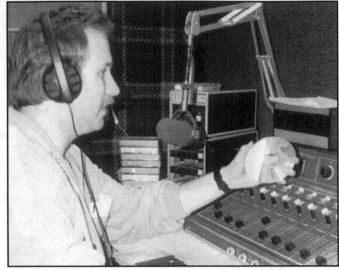

"Math is used every day in this business. So it was either learn it or don't work here." The voice is Rick Armon, disc jockey, chief operator, engineer, and announcer at WDLB Radio in Marshfield.

"I was terrible at math in school, because I didn't see any practical application for what I was learning. Algebra made no sense. Trigonometry made no sense. … When it's just numbers, it means nothing. But when you get a chance to use those numbers in real life, they become more than numbers. They become really interesting."

In Mr. Armon's job, knowing a system's voltage, current, resistance, and power are all crucial to getting off a good broadcast, and all three factors are related to each other in what we call Ohm's Law. Ohm's Law can take many forms, as shown on the chart.

Mr. Armon uses the formulas to find either voltage (E), current (I), resistance (R), or power (P) when he knows two of those four measurements. To find resistance, for example, he will choose a formula extending from the inner circle R. To find current, he chooses one of the three formulas extending from the I. Let's see if we can help Mr. Armon.

+ - x √ π ± ÷ ≥ + - x √ π ± ÷ ≥

- It might happen this way. I'm covering the Marshfield Tigers State Basketball Tournament in Madison, and I've got 20 minutes to set up. The fans are filling up the stadium, and suddenly I'm getting no power to my telephone remote. I could be in real trouble here.

  I check the power supply, because they have a tendency to fail first. I know this remote telephone has a resistance of 250 Ohms, and I measure the current at 0.25 amps.

  Now I've got to calculate if the voltage is where it's supposed to be. How do I do that?

- Another time I'm at the Marshfield Mall, covering the arrival of a major rock band, and I find my mixer board is asleep. I'm not getting anything. My Ohm meter doesn't tell me the voltage. With 20 minutes until air time, I know the power output is 50 watts and my resistance is 1 Ohm.

  Can I figure my voltage?

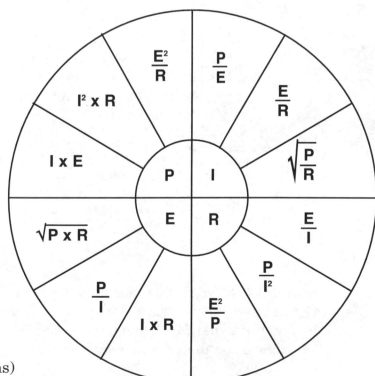

E = Voltage (volts)
I = Current (amps)
R = Resistance (Ohms)
P = Power (watts)

MARSHFIELD
• The City in the Center •

"When everybody's healthy, I'm happy," says Jim Hlavac, referring to the 265 birds and mammals in his charge.

As zookeeper of Wildwood Park Zoo, Mr. Hlavac tries to keep his animals in as natural and comfortable a setting as possible, and to look after each one's special needs. For a dedicated worker like Mr. Hlavac, that means contacting grocery stores to request leftover watermelon (which the bears adore), or tomatoes ("The elk *love* tomatoes").

And, as you may have guessed, Mr. Hlavac is required to make many decisions involving math.

+ - x √ π ± ÷ ≥ + - x √ π ± ÷ ≥

Last June, for example, four gibbons named Rich, Sammy, Goblin, and Egon came to live under Mr. Hlavac's care. The instructions that Mr. Hlavac received from the Brookfield Zoo in Chicago prescribed the following daily diet for the four gibbons:

GIBBON DAILY DIET

a.m. 1/2 can Science Diet   p.m. 3 cups HiPro chow

2 slices bread   210 g. green beans

1/2 c. peanuts   210 g. celery

1/2 c. raisins   1/2 c. sunflower seeds

200 g. apple   270 g. orange

90 g. banana   270 g. banana

2 c. grapes   143 g. sweet potato

                                           147 g. carrot

                                           73 g. onion

                                           20 g. parsley

                                           105 g. kale

                                           150 g. spinach

                                           380 g. lettuce

Mr. Hlavac checked into buying a scale to measure all these quantities, but found that the scale they needed would cost $1,600—way outside his budget. So he did the next best thing. He borrowed a scale from the vet. The only trouble was, it only measured in pounds and ounces. What to do?

- **Change the metric quantities listed into ounces.**

Use your calculator and round to the nearest ounce. How many ounces in a gram, or grams in an ounce? Look it up. Mr. Hlavac did. (A dictionary is one place to look.)

Problem Solving Strategy: Your Calculator is Your Friend

The memory on a calculator can help you keep track of a number you might otherwise forget. Here's how it works. Before you begin, be sure your calculator's memory is clear by pressing MRC and then M-. Push ON/C to be sure everything is cleared to zero, and then follow the steps below.
- Push "M+" to add any number to memory.
- Push "ON/C" once to return to the main keypad.
- ("M" will indicate you have something stored in memory)
- Enter the next number and the operation you wish done.
- Push "MRC" to retrieve the stored number.
- Push the = to find the answer.

Try these steps first using simpler numbers before trying Mr. Hlavac's problem.

KEN WEIS ELECTRIC, INC.
Electrical Contractor
Farm   -   Home   -   Commercial
Marshfield, Wis. 54449

Mark A Heintz

Dean Weis

Mark Heintz and Dean Weis are electricians for Ken Weis Electric.

According to Mr. Weis: "How do we use math? It takes some thinking to realize just how much math we do use in our jobs. As you notice, we've all got our measuring tapes on us. We use math all the time figuring out how big wires should be, how much load we can throw on a breaker, the amps/voltage/power output. And the conduit sizing is all different—that's all math."

+ - x √ π ± ÷ ≥ + - x √ π ± ÷ ≥

Here's an example from Mr. Heintz:

Lots of times the blueprints don't give you all the dimensions you need, and you have to calculate the unknowns.

Just the other day I was in a new building that was going up, and I had to mark the place for an outlet for a water fountain which was going to be installed. The blueprint I had only showed the dimension of the box from the drainpipe; so I had to calculate the distance from the floor. This is a rough drawing of what I had from the blueprint.

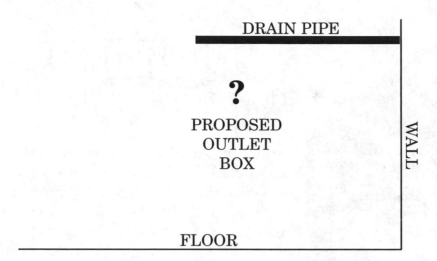

I did know that the exact center of the outlet box should be 1⁷/₈ inches to the left of the end of the drain pipe and 4⁷/₁₆ inches down from it. But the contractor had asked me to write down the distance from bottom of the outlet box to the floor.

The first thing I did was to measure the distance from the drain pipe to the floor and found it to be 25". I knew the outlet box would be 3³/₄" tall.

- **How far is it from the bottom edge of the outlet box to the floor?**

FIRE & RESCUE DEPARTMENT

Bernie Binning is a lieutenant with the Marshfield Fire Department. In his 25 years with the department, he's answered more than 3,000 fire calls. As Lieutenant Binning explains, there's a lot more to fighting fires than simply hooking a truck up to a hydrant and holding on to a hose.

"Water evaporates at 212° F. Some fires can burn at 1,200° F or hotter. So how do we keep the water from evaporating? We have to pour it on at a rate fast enough to absorb the heat. Without heat, the fire goes out. We call this rate the critical flow … and that's how fire fighters put out fires."

+ - x √ π ± ÷ ≥ + - x √ π ± ÷ ≥

- Now let's imagine a three-story building on fire. We know the building measures about 50' x 100', and half of it is already burning.

  Use the formula below to find the minimum number of gallons per minute we need to pour on the fire.
  Critical Flow= (length x width) ÷ (3) x (# stories) x (% involved)

- Now we need to figure how many fire fighters we'll need. On average, a firefighter can handle 50 gallons of water per minute. With 30 full-time firefighters in the Marshfield Fire Department, **will we have enough people to cover the fire? Or, if we have to send out for support, what is the minimum number of fire fighters we will need to request?**

- Next, our 2½" hand-held hoses deliver 250 gallons per minute.

   If you remember the critical flow you calculated, you can figure how many hoses you'll need.

- Now to get the waterstream to reach the fire is another math problem. For a straight stream of water, we need 50 pounds of pressure at the nozzle. The problem is, there is some loss of pressure as the water travels down the hose due to friction, and of course there is more friction loss with a longer hose.

Use the formula below to determine friction loss.

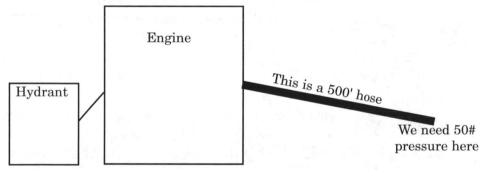

$$\text{Friction Loss} = (2 \times Q^2 + Q) \times L$$

Q = number of 100 gallons/minute per hose

L = each 100' of hose.

- **Now find how many pounds of pressure we have to deliver from the engine, adding 5 pounds for each extra story.**

Do firefighters really help cats out of trees?

"No, we don't do that anymore. It ties up manpower and resources. Besides … when's the last time you saw a cat skeleton in a tree?"

MARSHFIELD AREA

YMCA

410 W. McMillan Street, Marshfield, WI 54449 (715) 387-4900

Michael F. McLellan

As program director for the second fastest growing YMCA in the country, Mike McLellan must be doing something right. But it wasn't long ago that he was in school and struggling with math. "When I was growing up I was just so bad at math. I guess it was so easy to use the excuse, 'What are we ever going to use this for?' Now I know. We use it every day."

At the Y, even deciding whether or not to raise the temperature in the pool 2 degrees involves a great deal of mathematics. "Besides the additional cost of heat, we have to look at the cost of additional chemicals which will be needed when the water is warmer, and the possibility of the need for more staffing as more people use it. And then we have to decide whether the additional cost will be covered by the programs which use it."

+ - x √ π ± ÷ ≥ + - x √ π ± ÷ ≥

- Our computer helps us make those decisions. When members check in to the YMCA, they scan their card at the front desk. The scanner is connected to the computer, which keeps a record of their attendance. However, on any given day, about 20% of the Y members who come have forgotten their cards, and so their attendance is not recorded in the computer. We'd like to be able to estimate the percentage of

Marshfield YMCA members who use the Y on a daily basis. We know there are 6,143 total members.

Can we estimate that percentage from the information on this computer printout?

MARSHFIELD YMCA
Total Usage During March 1994

6 a.m.	463	12 p.m.	543	6 p.m.	1, 920
7 a.m.	559	1 p.m.	970	7 p.m.	1,263
8 a.m.	851	2 p.m.	908	8 p.m.	614
9 a.m.	683	3 p.m.	1,522	9 p.m.	192
10 a.m.	579	4 p.m.	1,467	10 p.m.	14
11 a.m.	596	5 p.m.	1,550		

• **How else might Mr. McLellan use these statistics?**

+ - x √ π ± ÷ ≥ + - x √ π ± ÷ ≥

"I really wish when I was growing up I had a chance to learn about statistics. Just about everything we do involves statistics."

Problem Solving Strategy: Let's Talk About It

When is the best time for Mr. McLellan to offer adult classes? Kids' classes? When should the Y offer babysitting? During what continuous four hours should the building supervisor be on duty? What time should the YMCA close at night? What time should it open in the morning? (Don't expect there to be only one right answer. Remember, this is real life.)

Marshfield
News-Herald

Bill Heath is the editor of Marshfield's daily newspaper.

"We use a lot of math in producing each day's issue of the *News-Herald*. I'll introduce you to some of the problems we face, but first you have to understand a few terms. In the newspaper world, we talk about how *deep* a story or picture runs. That means how many inches long it is vertically. *Cutlines* are the captions under pictures. *Display ads* are bigger ads which sometimes contain pictures of items on sale. *Classified ads* are the smaller ads, which sometimes advertise job openings or garage sales. Each page has 129 inches of vertical space, 3 columns wide."

+ - x √ π ± ÷ ≥ + - x √ π ± ÷ ≥

- In this issue we are going to use 50 inches for advertising. We plan to include a 3-column picture with a depth of 5 inches and a cutline that will require 3 total inches of space.

  How much room will we have left on the page for other stories and headlines?

- Today's issue has 492 inches of display advertising and 566 inches of classified advertising. We are going to produce a 20-page newspaper. Each page has 129 vertical inches of space to fill.

How many inches will we have for news and what will the percentage of news to advertising be?

- We have an $6\frac{7}{16}$ x 10 inch picture. We have to reduce that down to fill a three-column space. We need to reduce the picture to 6 inches wide.

What percentage of the original will achieve the required photo width?

Problem Solving Strategy: Draw a Diagram

There's no substitute for a picture to help clarify a problem.

+ - x √ π ± ÷ ≥ + - x √ π ± ÷ ≥

"Good luck with these problems."

As assistant city engineer, Rich Kaczmarowski is the designer for any new streets in the City of Marshfield. Drainage of runoff water presents one of the simpler problems Mr. Kaczmarowski and his crew face.

"We begin, as you might guess, by measuring elevations. Marshfield has a system of bench marks, which are points of known elevation above sea level, throughout the city.

"The tools used to find the elevation of a new bench mark are a level and a rod. The level (pictured) is essentially a telescope on a tripod. The level is called a level because it indicates when it is set up perfectly horizontally. Objects seen through it when it is perfectly horizontal are at the same elevation as the horizontal crosshair inside the telescope.

Problem Solving Strategy: Use Simpler Numbers

Having trouble visualizing this problem? Begin by rounding the numbers in the problem to the nearest foot. After you understand and can visualize the problem, work through it using the real numbers.

"The rod (not shown) is like an extra tall yard stick, marked boldly in hundreths of a foot with 0.00' at the bottom and 5.00' or more at the top."

To find a new elevation takes two people. One surveyor sets up the level and looks through the telescope. Through it, he or she reads the marking on the rod, which the other surveyor holds vertically on a known bench mark off in the distance. A second reading is then taken with the rod set on a new yet-to-be-determined bench mark. By comparing the two readings, Mr. Kaczmarowski and his crew can determine the elevation of the ground at the new bench mark.

+ - x √ π ± ÷ ≥ + - x √ π ± ÷ ≥

- Standing on a clear spot, looking through the level at a rod held at benchmark #2, Mr. Kaczmarowski reads 5.17 feet on the rod.

Which is higher, the crosshair inside Mr. Kaczmarowski's level, or the bench mark on which the rod is held?

Mr. Kaczmarowski knows bench mark #2 is marked with an elevation of 1250.75 feet above sea level. His partner then moves the rod to bench mark #470, and Mr. Kaczmarowski, still standing at where he was, observes a reading of 4.36 feet.

- **Which is higher, bench mark #2 or bench mark #470?**

- **What is the elevation above sea level of bench mark #470?**

> ### Problem Solving Strategy: Construct a Model
>
> **Make a model of this problem using a flat table, a ruler as a rod, and a table piled with books to create various elevations. Each book can stand for one foot of elevation if you wish. A cardboard tube with toothpicks poked through horizontally and vertically can serve as a level.**

+ - x √ π ± ÷ ≥ + - x √ π ± ÷ ≥

"In ten years, this will all be done through the use of satellites," he predicts. By the way, even though Mr. Kaczmarowski oversees all new street construction, don't look for him in his car. An avid cyclist, he uses his car only in the Wisconsin weather.

Perkins
sports inc.

Denny Reidel has been a part-owner of Perkins Sports for 16 years. Perkins sells everything from rollerblades to rappelling gear, from tennis rackets to trail food, and from BMX bikes to boomerangs. At Perkins, says Denny, "Everything we do involves numbers … it just becomes second nature.

"Precision is what math is all about, and precision is essential to the accurate adjustment of ski bindings. Downhill skiers need their bindings set to release if, and only if, they take a bad fall. A ski that doesn't release from a boot can cause serious injury. On the other hand, a ski that releases when you don't want it to can also cause trouble."

• Today Jake just bought his first pair of skis here at Perkins Sports. Jake skis slowly and cautiously. He weighs close to 200 pounds, he's 6 feet tall, and 52 years old. His ski boots are 330mm long.

Later in the afternoon, Jake's son Ethan comes in to get his skis adjusted. I know Ethan is a hotshot skier. I've seen him fly over moguls. Ethan is tall and slender, 5'11" and 128 pounds. He wears the same size boots as his dad.

According to the Marker© binding adjustment chart, whose bindings should be set tighter, Ethan's or his dad's?

Skier Weight	Skier Height	Skier Code	Toe and Heal Setting Indicator Value						Release Torque Range					
			Boot Sole Length						Twist			Forward Lean		
			1	2	3	4	5	6	min.	ref.	max.	min.	ref.	max.
Pounds	Ft. In.		≤250mm	251-270mm	271-290mm	291-310mm	331-330mm	≥331mm		5			18	
22-29		A	0,75	0,75					5	8	11	19	29	39
30-38		B	1	1	0,75				8	11	14	30	40	50
39-47		C	1,25	1,25	1				11	14	17	42	52	62
48-56		D	1,75	1,5	1,5				14	17	20	54	64	74
57-66		E	2	2	1,75				17	20	23	65	75	85
67-78		F	2,5	2,5	2,25	2	1,75	1,75	20	23	26	77	87	97
79-91		G		3	2,5	2,5	2,25	2	24	27	30	92	102	112
92-107	4'10"	H		3,5	3	3	2,5	2,5	28	31	34	108	120	132
108-125	4'11"-5'1"	I		4,25	4	3,5	3,25	3,25	33	37	41	127	141	155
126-147	5'2"-5'5"	J		5	4,75	4,5	4	4	39	43	47	148	165	182
148-174	5'6"-5'10"	K		6	5,5	5,25	5	4,75	45	50	55	175	194	213
175-209	5'11"-6'4"	L		7	6,75	6,25	6	5,75	52	58	64	206	229	252
210+	6'5"+	M		8,5	8	7,5	7	6,75	60	67	74	244	271	298
		N		10	9,5	9,0	8,5	8,25	70	78	86	288	320	352
		O		12	11,25	10,75	10,25	10	82	91	100	342	380	418

Determine the type of skier, from one of the following groups:

I—Cautious skiing at lighter release/retention settings. Skiers who designate themselves "I" must accept a narrower margin of retention in order to gain a wider margin of release.

II—Average/moderate skiing at average release/retention settings. Skiers who designate themselves "II" must accept a balanced compromise between release and retention.

III—Aggressive, higher speed skiing at higher release/retention settings. Skiers who designate themselves "III" must accept a narrower margin or release in order to gain a wider margin of retention.

Step 1
Find the Release Code (letter A through O) which corresponds to the skier's weight, as well as the release code which corresponds to the skier's height. If they are not the same, choose the one that is closer to the top of the chart.

Step 2
Make adjustments for skier type and age. The selection from step 1 is for a "I" type skier. If the skier type is "II" move down the chart one code. If the skier type is "III" move down two codes. If the skier is over 50, move up the chart one code.

Step 3
Reading on the corrected release code line from step 2, find the column with the skier's boot length. Within the box which corresponds to the skier's release code and boot length is a number. Use this number for Maker models.

- **If a person is short and stocky, should I choose the measurement for height or for weight? Why?**

- **Why does a person's height affect how tightly his or her bindings need to be set?**

Problem Solving Strategy: Let's Talk About It

Perhaps someone with downhill skiing experience can add to the class' understanding of this problem.

+ - x √ π ± ÷ ≥ + - x √ π ± ÷ ≥

Problem Solving Strategy: Use Simpler Numbers

Since the customer only wants an estimate, we can round the cost of each cable to $3, remembering that the actual cost will be a little more. Figuring the 5% tax is simple if you first find 10%, then cut it in half.

Brian Hansen is a bike specialist for Perkins Sports. The customer who brought in this bike is waiting for an estimate. Brian looks over the bike, figures out what it needs, and then calculates the customer's estimated cost in his head.

Brian knows this bike will need four new cables, and that each cable will cost $3.06 in parts. He also knows it will take 15 minutes to install each cable, and Perkins' labor charge is $16.00 per hour. Then he figures the 5% tax, adds it to his previous total, and rounds it to the nearest dollar. Then Brian adds a couple dollars to cover any unexpected work which he may find later the bike needs.

- **Like Brian, mentally calculate the estimate for this job.**

OF MARSHFIELD

Tamera Schecklman is the service representative at Valley Sanitation, Marshfield's recycling center. Ms. Schecklman says, "Not only is math an important part of life in general, it is a *very* important part of everyone's job at Valley Sanitation."

AUTHOR'S NOTE: Although it is certainly more convenient to use a calculator or paper and pencil, it is time to increase your mental math powers! For that reason, don't use paper, pencil or calculators for these questions. Write down the answers only. Calculate only mentally. You can do it.

+ - x √ π ± ÷ ≥ + - x √ π ± ÷ ≥

- Every time a garbage truck comes in to empty we weigh the truck on our outdoor scale. The truck then goes down into the transfer station and empties out the garbage, then stops back on the scale so we can get an empty weight.

  If the truck weighed in at 37,910 pounds, and weighed out at 26,090 pounds, how many tons of garbage would the truck have had on it? (There are 2,000 pounds in a ton.)

- We have several different sizes of dumpsters that we rent to our customers. When our customers call, we ask them what size dumpster they would like. The smallest dumpster we have holds 6 cubic yards of garbage. We tell the customer that the price on the dumpster is $20 per cubic yard.

If the customer put 6 cubic yards of garbage in the dumpster weekly, and he or she is billed four times a year, how much would he or she be charged on one bill?

- All of our customers have certain days on which their garbage gets picked up. If they call in and want it picked up on a different day, we have to charge them mileage. Our rate is $1.25 per mile round-trip.

If a customer calls and says that he or she needs garbage picked up right away, and he or she lives eight miles from Valley Sanitation, how much would we charge?

- At Valley Sanitation right now we are paying 20¢ per pound for aluminum brought in.

What do we pay a customer who brings in 43 pounds of aluminum cans, and 62 pounds of aluminum scrap material?

- At the end of every day I go through and add up all of the pounds of garbage that our garbage trucks bring in, so I can see exactly how much garbage we took in that day. I also do this at the end of each week so I can get a weekly total. Last Wednesday these were all of the weights in pounds.

<u>Wednesday's Garbage</u>

9,390	12,140
19,600	6,420
15,170	690
14,360	12,210
11,850	

How many pounds of garbage did we take in last
Wednesday?

• How many tons did we take in last Wednesday (to the
nearest ton)?

+ - x √ π ± ÷ ≥ + - x √ π ± ÷ ≥

"That was just a little taste of the math that I do every day on
my job. Hope you have fun solving these problems!"

ANTHROPOLOGICAL STUDIES INSTITUTE
UNIVERSITY OF WISCONSIN-STEVENS POINT
STEVENS POINT, WI 54481

John H. Moore

What is the square root of 2, and why does it matter to an archeologist?

Ask John Moore, archeologist, professor of anthropology, and director of the eight-county Regional Archeology Center in Central Wisconsin. Mr. Moore's work in the field often has him scouring the hillsides around Marshfield, looking for remains of ancient native American cultures. Every step of his work involves mathlike precision—every shovelful of dirt has to be sifted, notations must be made on every layer of earth removed, and every artifact—whether spearpoint or pottery fragment—must be carefully photographed, recorded, and stored.

"Precision is essential to archeology. We may finish digging in an area and want to return to that spot years later. As you know, one clump of dirt looks pretty much like another. So before we ever begin an excavation, we work out an accurate measurement of the location, within 1 centimeter degree of accuracy.

"The archeologist only excavates one square meter at a time. And keeping a square meter square is harder than it looks. Even a slight error in angle or measure can be multiplied into a very large error as the archeologist works across a wide area." For that reason, Mr. Moore and his fellow archeologists meticulously measure and remeasure the diagonal ($a^2 + b^2 = c^2$) of each square meter before ever putting their shovels into the ground.

+ - x √ π ± ÷ ≥ + - x √ π ± ÷ ≥

Mr. Moore has just marked with string this 1 meter x 1 meter plot.

- **Without using a calculator, find out how many centimeters he hopes its diagonal measurement will read (to the nearest centimeter).**

$$+ - \times \sqrt{} \pi \pm \div \geq + - \times \sqrt{} \pi \pm \div \geq$$

"When I was first introduced to archeology, I never thought it would involve money, accounting and budgets; I figured you just went out and did it. Now I am keenly aware of the fact that accounting and budgeting is the backbone of the whole process—without it the excavations would never be possible."

With the $15,000 biannual allotment provided to the Regional Archeology Center by the State of Wisconsin, Mr. Moore develops a six-month budget. There are a number of factors he must consider:

✔ Because it is housed in the science building on campus, the center must pay 5% of its allotment to the university for rent, heat, and electricity.

✔ He will budget $6,500 for salaries. Of that, $3,500 will go toward his salary, and the rest for students whom he will hire for field and lab work.

✔ He knows he should set aside $2,500 for services and supplies, and another $3,500 for miscellaneous concerns which will arise. The rest can be used for travel.

✔ The Archeology Center's 16-passenger van costs 63¢ per mile to operate, and the present Marshfield excavation site is 34 miles from the Regional Archeology Center.

$+ - \times \sqrt{} \pi \pm \div \geq + - \times \sqrt{} \pi \pm \div \geq + - \times \sqrt{} \pi \pm \div \geq + - \times \sqrt{} \pi \pm \div \geq + - \times \sqrt{} \pi \pm$

Real Life Math Mysteries   **47**

- How many students can he hire to work 4 hours a day, 5 days a week for 10 weeks at a cost to the center of $7.50 an hour?

- What is the maximum number of miles that he should plan to travel in the six-month period and, based on this budget, how many trips to the site in Marshfield would that allow?

K. Mitchell

MARSHFIELD CLINIC

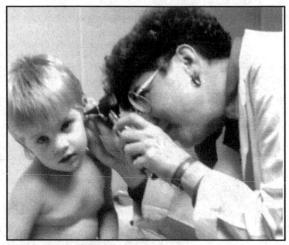

As a pediatric nurse practitioner, Karen Mitchell is responsible for the health of a great many babies and children. And she uses math every day.

Let's follow Ms. Mitchell on her rounds.

+ - x √ π ± ÷ ≥ + - x √ π ± ÷ ≥

- Kimberly has an ear infection and she needs to be put on Amoxicillin. The dosage for this medicine is 40mg per kilogram of body weight, and that amount is divided into three daily doses. Kimberly weighs 24 pounds.

   How many mg of Amoxicillin should she receive per dose? (To convert pounds to kilograms, divide by 2.2)

- Amoxicillin is given as a liquid, and 250 mg = 5 liquid ml.

   How many ml should Kimberly receive per dose (to the nearest whole number)?

- Newborns can lose up to 10% of their body weight before we worry that they are becoming dehydrated and we need to consider supplementing breastfeeding with formula. Joey weighed 6 lb. 12 oz. when he was born, but began losing weight. His weight three days after his birth is 6 lb. 4 oz.

   Do we need to consider supplemental feedings?

+ - x √ π ± ÷ ≥ + - x √ π ± ÷ ≥

"The people in my nursing school class who didn't have a strong math background really struggled."

AS AVIATION SERVICES, INC.

Walter Embke

"There's always something to work on in flying. If the landing is a little rough, you think, next time I'll do it better, and there's a feeling of satisfaction when you do. ... Flying is a skill we are always perfecting."

Those are interesting words coming from Walter Embke, chief pilot for Aviation Services, a man who has accumulated enough hours in the air to have flown an airplane to the moon and back 10 times! In 37 years of piloting, Mr. Embke has seen many changes in the airplane industry, including the development of computerized and radar navigation techniques.

"A lot of the math in flying has been taken care of by computers. What's left is more like common sense. You see, pilots can't rely on our gauges all the time—gauges break. So I have to continually monitor the gauges to see that they are checking out to what is expected, and I have to be sure I have enough fuel to continue if the weather causes a deviation from the flight plan. These are mathematical calculations, and the pilot has to have an almost subconscious feel for these things.

"To think like a pilot, you need to know a few aviation terms. For us, 0° refers to straight north, 90° refers to east, 180° south, etc. And you need to know that pilots measure our air speed in knots per hour. Knots are nautical miles, which are 15% larger than your normal statute mile."

$+ - \times \sqrt{} \pi \pm \div \geq + - \times \sqrt{} \pi \pm \div \geq$

$+ - \times \sqrt{} \pi \pm \div \geq + - \times \sqrt{} \pi \pm \div \geq + - \times \sqrt{} \pi \pm \div \geq + - \times \sqrt{} \pi \pm \div \geq + - \times \sqrt{} \pi \pm$

50   Real Life Math Mysteries

- Let's say some people wanted to charter your Cessna to Minneapolis. (Maybe they wanted to go to the *Mall of America*.) Minneapolis is directly west of Marshfield, so we set our true course at 270°. Now let's say there is a wind blowing from 90° at 10 knots. Normally this plane travels at 100 knots per hour, but a wind like that will affect our speed.

  How fast will we travel, and how long will it take us to fly the 150 statute miles to Minneapolis?
  (Hint: statute miles divided by 1.15 = nautical miles)

- As the pilot, you have to make sure your plane is not over-loaded. Here are some things you've got to consider:

  The manufacturer specifies that this Cessna's maximum weight is 2,650 pounds. Its empty weight is 1,650 pounds. The two male passengers boarding weigh 172 and 218 pounds respectively; the two female passengers weigh in at 136 and 202 pounds. The passengers' combined baggage weighs 190 pounds.

  There's one more thing you can't forget … the weight of your fuel. This plane averages 9 gallons per hour, but you must also carry an additional 45 minutes worth of fuel in the reserve for safety reasons. A gallon of fuel weighs 6 pounds.

  The question is, can this plane carry this weight to Minneapolis? I'll need a complete report.

MARSHFIELD
· *The City in the Center* ·

Mayor Richard Daniels uses plenty of math in his job overseeing city government.

"Our job in politics is to analyze statistics that tell us how things are, decide if we need to make any adjustments in the way things are done, and then communicate these ideas to the public. That's the tricky part—to translate raw statistics into something the public can understand.

"In Marshfield, we have a problem. The City of Marshfield is one of the highest taxed cities in the state, and the State of Wisconsin is one of the highest taxed states in the country. That isn't all. We have increasing needs that will require more money in the future. We don't want to raise taxes. What should we do?"

"There are only two ways to tackle a problem like this.
1. We can increase the amount of money we bring in.
2. We can cut the cost of city government.

"Increasing the amount of money we bring in without raising taxes won't be easy. One reason Marshfield's taxes are so high already is that a lot of the land in Marshfield is tax exempt. Research centers, churches, and hospitals are not required to pay city taxes, and a good portion of Marshfield is composed of these properties. The services we provide to these landowners in the way of police and fire protection, water and electrical lines are all paid for by the relatively few property owners who are required to pay taxes. I'm working on this matter now.

"The second method of solving our problem—cutting the cost of city government—maybe you can help me with. By making

City	Pop.	City-Purpose Property Tax Rate Amt.	Rank	City	Pop.	City-Purpose Property Tax Rate Amt.	Rank	City	Pop.	City-Purpose Property Tax Rate Amt.	Rank
Abbotsford	1,950	$6.89	134	Greenfield	34,549	8.70	84	Onalaska	12,569	7.48	120
Adams	1,738	9.56	48	Greenwood	980	7.86	107	Oshkosh	56,541	8.23	95
Algoma	3,348	11.63	13	Hartford	8,489	8.44	90	Osseo	1,554	8.92	75
Alma	847	3.03	188	Hayward	1,899	7.88	106	Owen	922	6.70	139
Altoona	6,145	7.97	103	Hillsboro	1,330	9.94	34	Park Falls	3,109	9.08	69
Amery	2,708	8.49	88	Horicon	3,897	8.28	93	Peshtigo	3,201	3.36	187
Antigo	8,432	6.24	151	Hudson	6,608	7.65	114	Phillips	1,630	9.74	43
Appleton	66,658	10.99	18	Hurley	1,796	10.98	19	Pittsville	840	9.19	63
Arcadia	2,176	6.54	143	Independence	1,060	9.55	49	Platteville	9,946	6.08	157
Ashland	8,667	12.47	6	Janesville	53,358	7.82	109	Plymouth	6,917	6.16	156
Augusta	1,523	12.68	3	Jefferson	6,135	6.80	138	Port Wash.	9,610	7.75	110
Baraboo	9,523	9.73	45	Juneau	2,132	7.29	126	Portage	8,800	9.43	53
Barron	3,070	5.58	164	Kaukauna	12,132	8.45	89	Pr. du Chien	5,722	6.36	148
Bayfield	684	12.08	7	Kenosha	82,203	9.87	38	Prescott	3,333	8.91	76
Beaver Dam	14,590	9.03	73	Kewaunee	2,757	8.81	80	Princeton	1,469	7.98	102
Beloit	35,621	10.74	23	Kiel	2,973	3.96	185	Racine	84,891	14.88	2
Berlin	5,377	10.93	20	La Crosse	51,335	9.07	70	Reedsburg	6,039	9.06	71
Bl. River Fls.	3,576	7.39	123	Ladysmith	4,002	5.59	163	Rhinelander	7,430	11.72	10
Blair	1,129	7.42	122	Lake Geneva	6,161	7.51	119	Rice Lake	8,023	10.23	30
Bloomer	3,191	8.17	99	Lake Mills	4,256	6.83	135	Richland Cnrt.	5,034	8.59	87
Boscobel	2,741	9.31	57	Lancaster	4,197	8.28	92	Ripon	7,328	5.96	158
Brillion	2,843	5.60	162	Lodi	2,226	7.63	115	River Falls	10,683	6.80	137
Brodhead	3,151	8.62	85	Loyal	1,234	9.53	51	St. Croix Falls	1,643	5.73	160
Brookfield	35,795	5.48	168	Madison	194,591	10.31	29	St. Francis	9,221	10.10	33
Burralo City	927	4.84	179	Manawa	1,221	9.20	62	Schofield	2,420	7.83	108
Burlington	8,975	8.95	74	Manitoc	33,278	7.37	124	Seymour	2,846	9.73	44
Cedarburg	10,195	7.99	101	Marinette	11,861	11.03	17	Shawano	7,645	6.55	142
Chetek	1,955	5.71	161	Marion	1,241	9.23	61	Sheboygan	49,684	10.53	27
Chilton	3242	4.85	178	Markesan	1,519	7.20	128	Sheb. Falls	5,910	3.85	186
Cheppewa Fls.	12,838	9.89	37	**Marshfield**	**19,630**	**11.68**	**11**	Shell Lake	1,195	8.21	96
Clintonville	4,478	10.22	31	Mauston	3,480	11.29	16	Shullsburg	1,240	5.11	173
Colby	1,556	5.51	167	Mayville	4,515	6.24	154	S. Milwuakee	21,040	9.18	64
Columbus	4,159	8.62	86	Medford	4,318	4.51	182	Sparta	7,873	7.48	121
Cornell	1,546	7.26	127	Mellen	973	6.62	141	Spooner	2,500	7.01	132
Crandon	1,977	6.66	140	Menasha	14,928	10.65	25	Stanley	2,028	11.81	9
Cuba City	2,029	5.42	169	Menominie	13,608	7.73	111	Stevens Point	23,188	9.72	46
Cudahy	18,686	8.70	83	Mequon	20,161	5.19	172	Stoughton	9,323	5.76	159
Cumberland	2,188	7.95	104	Merrill	10,148	10.54	26	Sturgeon Bay	9,254	9.74	42
Darlington	2,258	9.15	67	Middleton	14,160	6.89	133	Sun Prairie	16,070	7.56	117
DePere	16,923	10.75	22	Milton	4,555	6.27	150	Superior	27,263	10.86	21
Delafield	5,598	4.97	177	Milwaukee	629,554	11.55	14	Thorp	1,680	6.52	146
Delavan	6,191	5.29	171	Mineral Pt.	2,431	10.37	28	Tomah	7,756	9.53	50
Dodgeville	4,008	8.18	98	Mondovi	2,503	6.54	144	Tomahawk	3,336	9.26	59
Durand	1,996	5.55	165	Monona	8,579	6.46	147	Two Rivers	13,124	8.19	97
Eagle River	1,377	15.12	1	Monroe	10,298	9.27	58	Verona	5,595	7.13	130
Eau Clair	57,403	7.05	131	Montello	1,361	4.75	180	Viroqua	3,955	7.67	113
Edgerton	4,276	8.72	82	Montreal	845	7.53	118	Washburn	2,280	9.16	65
Elkhorn	5,865	7.68	112	Mosinee	3,898	6.24	153	Waterloo	2,746	7.16	129
Elroy	1,549	8.27	94	Muskego	17,704	4.54	181	Watertown	19,637	8.89	78
Evansville	3,226	9.09	68	Neenah	23,400	9.50	52	Waukesha	58,113	9.35	56
Fennimore	2,432	6.24	152	Neillsville	2,687	9.84	40	Waupaca	5,185	11.66	12
Fitchburg	16,254	5.05	174	Nekoosa	2,634	12.50	4	Waupun	9,150	8.33	91
Fond du Lac	38,589	9.91	36	New Berlin	34,342	5.03	176	Wausau	37,708	9.76	41
Fr. Atkinson	10,411	8.00	100	New Holstein	3,305	9.85	39	Wautoma	1,816	11.47	15
Fountain City	930	5.39	170	New Lisbon	1,506	7.31	125	Wauwatosa	49,484	8.89	77
Fox Lake	1,361	9.04	72	New London	6,747	8.77	81	W. Allis	63,374	10.13	32
Franklin	23,168	5.51	166	New Richmond	5,222	6.81	136	West Bend	25,374	9.40	54
Galesville	1,343	10.70	24	Niagra	2,017	9.26	60	Westby	1,898	7.59	116
Gillett	1,345	4.24	184	Oak Creek	20,543	9.15	66	Weyauwega	1,683	2.53	189
Glendale	14,101	6.52	145	Oconomowoc	11,192	6.17	155	Whitehall	1,534	4.35	183
Glenwood City	1,045	6.35	149	Oconto	4,464	8.84	79	Whitewater	12,823	5.05	175
Green Bay	97,801	9.94	35	Oconto Falls	2,594	7.94	105	Wis. Dells	2,382	12.04	8
Green Lake	1,082	9.37	55	Omro	2,849	9.60	47	Wis. Rapids	18,354	12.47	5

some wise adjustments, I hope we can reduce the tax burden for all Marshfield residents."

✔ Statistics show that the biggest chunk of our city government budget (62%) goes for the salary and fringe benefits of our city employees.

✔ Research has also shown that in Marshfield we are presently paying our city employees 30%-40% more than people who do similar jobs in private business. It seems to me there's something wrong there.

✔ I have provided some information I received from the Wisconsin Taxpayer Alliance. It shows the tax rate for a property owner in each city in the state of Wisconsin. It shows that a person who owns property in Marshfield paid $11.68 for every $1,000 worth of property he or she owned. Compared to other cities in Wisconsin, that's high.

"My problem now is to be able to communicate this data at the next Finance Committee meeting. I think they will be especially interested to see how Marshfield compares with Wausau and Stevens Point, which are close by. I'm going to need some good graphics."

• **Do you think you could help me come up with some convincing visuals to show the committee why we need to cut costs, particularly city employee salaries?**

May Ford Washington

Do writers use math? For sure.

Math creeps up in the strangest places. Trying to create the dedication for this book became for me a study of probability. It started with something like this:

DEDICATED TO MY CHILDREN
And I put their names in order of age:
CARMEN, CARRIE, ESTHER, AND DAVID

Then I thought, putting them in order of age may not be a good idea, because the oldest always seems to go first.

CARRIE, CARMEN, ESTHER, AND DAVID
This looked a little better, but I still didn't think it was fair that the two youngest should be last, because they're always last.

ESTHER, CARRIE, CARMEN, AND DAVID
Better, but David was still last.

ESTHER, CARRIE, DAVID AND CARMEN
This seemed better, but the oldest now had too much attention in the last place. I decided she should be stuck in the middle someplace.

ESTHER, CARMEN, DAVID, AND CARRIE
Better, but it seemed to me that David being the youngest should still be closer to the front.

ESTHER, DAVID, CARMEN, AND CARRIE
Well, maybe.

If the names can be in any order, how many possible combinations are there?

> **Problem Solving Strategy: Make A List of Possibilities; Work Systematically**

+ - x √ π ± ÷ ≥ + - x √ π ± ÷ ≥

Teacher's Guide to
Real Life Math Problems

+ - x √ π ± ÷ ≥ + - x √ π ± ÷ ≥

Answer Key Index

Real Life Math Problems

Answer Key

Associated Bank, page 2

- **What would I earn in interest over the entire 10-year period?**

A chart can help you to work systematically and keep track of where you are.

principle + interest = new balance

(remember to add $1,000 to savings each year)

end of 1st year:	$1,000.00 + (.08 x 1,000.00) = 1,080.00
end of 2nd year:	2,080.00 + (.08 x 2,080.00) = 2,246.40
end of 3rd year:	3,246.40 + (.08 x 3,246.40) = 3,506.11
end of 4th year:	4,506.11 + (.08 x 4,506.11) = 4,866.60
end of 5th year:	5,866.60 + (.08 x 5,866.60) = 6,335.93

Let's try this an easier way.

end of 6th year	7,335.93 x 1.08	= 7,922.80
end of 7th year	8,922.80 x 1.08	= 9,636.63
end of 8th year	10,636.63 x 1.08	=11,487.56
end of 9th year	12,487.56 x 1.08	=13,486.56
end of 10th year	14,486.56 x 1.08	=15,645.49

15,645.49 final balance
-10,000.00 put into savings
5,645.49 interest

You earned $5,645.49 interest.

- **How much interest will I have paid at the end of the three years?**

$161.34	$5,808.24
x 36 months	-5,000.00
$5,808.24	$ 808.24

You will have paid $808.24 in interest.

Schalow's Nursery, page 4

- **Knowing that there are 89 square feet of brick in a pallet, how many pallets will I need to order?**

<u>12 x 16 foot </u>brick patio = 192 square feet

192 ÷ 89 = 2.1573033 = ┌──────────────────┐
                        │ 3 pallets of bricks │
                        └──────────────────┘

- **How can we find out if the patio borders we have drawn are square with the house?**

a =16'
If P is a right angle, then:
$a^2 + b^2 = c^2$
$16^2 + 12^2 = c^2$
$256 + 144 = c^2$
$400 = c^2$

c will equal 20'

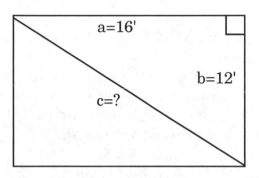

┌────────────────────────────────────┐
│   If the patio borders are square,   │
│ then the diagonal will measure 20' exactly. │
└────────────────────────────────────┘

- **Roses will be placed every 3 feet around the circumference of the 18' diameter pool. Each will be planted $1^1/2$' fro the edge. How many roses will we plant?**

circumference = π x d   c = 18 + $1^1/2$ + $1^1/2$ = 21
   circumference = 3.1417 x 18'   c = 3.14 x 21
   circumference = 56.55'   c = 65.94 = 66
   56.55' ÷ 3 = 18.85 roses   66 ÷ 3 = 22 roses

┌────────────────────────┐
│ We will plant 22 roses. │
└────────────────────────┘

Wildwood Animal Hospital, page 6

- **How often should the drip chamber drip in order to deliver the total (1,920 ml) in 24 hours?**

Twenty-four hours is a lot of drips, and it is hard to visualize.
Let's look at a more narrow range of time.
   1,920 ml ÷ 24 hours = 80 ml per hour
   80 ml per hour ÷ 60 minutes per hour = $1^1/3$ ml per minute
   $1^1/3$ x 15 drops per ml = 20 drops per minute

Can you visualize it dripping 20 drops per minute?
If you can, then you also know if your final answer makes sense.

60 seconds per minute ÷ 20 drops per minute = every 3 seconds

> It needs to drip every 3 seconds.

Marshfield Heart Care page 7

- **Do we have enough cardiologists to see the 30,000 patients we expect to see in Marshfield in the next year *and* have time to help out these other clinics in northern Wisconsin?**

```
   365 days in a year
 - 104 weekend days (52 x 2)
   261
  - 25 vacation days
   236
  - 12 education/meeting days
   224
  - 14 business/scientific days
   210 days each cardiologist available
```

210 days x 10 patients per day
= 2,100 patients per cardiologist per year

```
 2,100 patients              31,500 patients possible
   x 15 cardiologists       - 30,000 patients in Marshfield
31,500 patients yearly        1,500 patients available
```

> Yes, we have time available to help the other clinics.

- **If so, and this available time is divided equally among the staff, how many days would each doctor be available to assist other clinics?**

1,500 patient visits ÷ 10 patients per day = 150 staff days
150 days available ÷ 15 cardiologists = 10 days per cardiologist

> Each cardiologist will be available 10 days.

Pizza Hut, page 9

- **What's the minimum amount of lettuce I should order for next week?**

head lettuce:

Sunday	$2^3/_4$	=	$2^3/_4$
Monday	$1^3/_4$	=	$1^3/_4$
Tuesday	$1^1/_4$	=	$1^1/_4$
Wednesday	$1^1/_2$	=	$1^2/_4$
Thursday	$1^1/_2$	=	$1^2/_4$
Friday	$3^1/_2$	=	$3^2/_4$
Saturday	$3^1/_4$	=	$3^1/_4$

$12^{14}/_4 = 15^1/_4 = 16$ head lettuce

Romaine lettuce:

Sunday	$1^1/_2$	=	$1^2/_4$
Monday	$^1/_2$	=	$^2/_4$
Tuesday	$^1/_4$	=	$^1/_4$
Wednesday	1	=	1
Thursday	$^1/_2$	=	$^2/_4$
Friday	2	=	2
Saturday	$1^1/_4$	=	$1^1/_4$

$5^8/_4 = 7$ Romaine

> 15 head lettuce
> 7 Romaine

- **If a customer asks for the pizza to be half pepperoni/ cheese/mushroom and the other half double cheese/ mushroom, how much or how many of what cups of each color do we use?**

The recipe calls for:

pepperoni	1 red cup	x	$^1/_2$	=	$^1/_2$	red cup
mushrooms	1 green cup	x	1	=	1	green cup
cheese	1 blue cup	x	$1^1/_2$	=	$1^1/_2$	blue cup

> $^1/_2$ red cup pepperoni, 1 green cup mushrooms, $1^1/_2$ blue cups cheese

- **From what you see of last week's pizza sales, how many bundles of dough should I order to cover next week's hand-tossed pizzas?**

$+ - x \sqrt{} \pi \pm \div \geq + - x \sqrt{} \pi \pm \div \geq + - x \sqrt{} \pi \pm \div \geq + - x \sqrt{} \pi \pm \div \geq + - x \sqrt{} \pi \pm$

Real Life Math Mysteries   63

Answer Key

+ - x √ π ± ÷ ≥ + - x √ π ± ÷ ≥ + - x √ π ± ÷ ≥ + - x √ π ± ÷ ≥ + - x √ π ±

DAILY SALES: HAND-TOSSED PIZZAS

	THURS	FRI	SAT	SUN	MON	TUES	WED
SMALL	16	18	18	18	16	16	16
MEDIUM	24	29	29	29	24	24	24
LARGE	20	23	23	23	20	20	19

Total sales small pizzas: 118 ÷ 23 per bag = 5.13 bags
Total sales medium pizzas: 183 ÷ 13 per bag = 14.08 bags
Total sales large pizzas: 148 ÷ 8 per bag = 18.50 bags

Total :   37.71   = 38 bags

38 bags ÷ 4 per bundle = 9.5 bundles = 10 bundles

10 bundles + 2 extra = | 12 bundles of dough |

Juneau, Minder, Gross & Stevning-Roe, S.C., page 11

- **What will be the amount needed for the final payoff?**

Use your formula to figure the amount of interest which must be paid:

INTEREST = % INTEREST x TOTAL JUDGMENT x PERCENTAGE OF YEAR
12% x $20,000 x % of year

How do we figure the percent of a year? Count the days.
    31 days October
   - 8
    23 days October + 30 days November + 20 days December
         = 73 days

    73 days ÷ 365 = 0.20
    Percent of Year = 20%

Now go back to our formula:

    12% x $20,000 x 20%
    0.12 x 20,000 x 0.20 = $480 interest to be paid

+ - x √ π ± ÷ ≥ + - x √ π ± ÷ ≥ + - x √ π ± ÷ ≥ + - x √ π ± ÷ ≥ + - x √ π ±

Now what?

Besides interest, the person must pay the original judgment sum ($20,000) and fees. We can write a new formula:

FINAL PAYOFF = INTEREST + JUDGEMENT + FEES

abstractor fees	$130.00
filing fee	78.00
service fee	36.00
postage	27.00
photocopies	+ 33.00
	$304.00 total fees

Final payoff = 480 + 20,000 + 304

$$\boxed{\text{Final payoff} = \$20,784}$$

Now ask yourself: Is my answer logical? Does it make sense?

The Lucas Farm, page 12

How many bags of soybeans will I need to plant 10 acres?

250,000 seeds needed per acre x 10 acres = 2,500,000 seeds

Averaging roughly 2,700 and 2,592 (2,600) would yield 2,650 seeds per pound.

2,650	seeds per pound
x 50	pounds per bag
132,500	seeds per bag

2,500,000 seeds needed ÷ 132,500 seeds per bag = 18.87 = $\boxed{\text{19 bags}}$

How many plants can I expect to grow on the 10 acres?

2,500,000 seeds planted x .92 germination rate

$$\boxed{2,300,000 \text{ soy plants}}$$

$+ - \times \sqrt{} \ \pi \pm \div \geq + - \times \sqrt{} \ \pi \pm \div \geq + - \times \sqrt{} \ \pi \pm \div \geq + - \times \sqrt{} \ \pi \pm \div \geq + - \times \sqrt{} \ \pi \pm$

Real Life Math Mysteries   65

Answer Key

What is the maximum herd I can keep with a daily milk pick-up?

In order to figure when the tank will be full, we have to change pounds of milk to gallons. We know that a gallon weighs 8.5 pounds. There are fewer gallons than pounds, so we must divide to find gallons.

55 pounds per day ÷ 8.5 pounds per gallon
= 6.47 gallons per cow each day

415 gallons to fill the tank ÷ 6.47 gallons per cow = 64.14 cows

Maximum herd 64

Figure how many pounds of feed a cow giving 70 pounds of milk needs. Organizing the information into a table can help you think more clearly:

milk production	70	80	90	100
grain mix		27.1		25.7
hay		20.0		20.0
corn silage		25.0		31.2
protein, etc.		4.0		8.3

The next step might be to average the feed of an 80 and a 100-pound milk producer to find the 90 pound feed schedule.

27.1	25.0	4.0
+25.7	+ 31.2	+ 8.3
52.8	56.2	12.3

52.8 ÷ 2 = 26.4   56.2 ÷ 2 = 28.1   12.3 ÷ 2 = 6.15

milk production	70	80	90	100
grain mix		27.1	26.4	25.7
hay		20.0	20.0	20.0
corn silage		25.0	28.1	31.2
protein, etc.		4.0	6.2	8.3

If we find the difference between feeds for each weight, we will be able to find the feed schedule for a 70# milk producer.

27.1	27.1	28.1	25.0	6.2	4.0
- 26.4	+0.7	-25.0	- 3.1	- 4.0	-2.2
0.7	27.8	3.1	21.9	2.2	1.8

milk production	70	80	90	100
grain mix	27.8	27.1	26.4	25.7
hay	20.0	20.0	20.0	20.0
corn silage	21.9	25.0	28.1	31.2
protein, etc.	1.8	4.0	6.2	8.3

Side-Kix Taekwan-do, page 14

Can you calculate how many foot pounds of force were behind his punch?

Velocity = $\dfrac{\text{distance (feet)}}{\text{time (seconds)}}$

Velocity = $\dfrac{\text{distance (feet)}}{0.4 \text{ seconds} - 0.2 \text{ seconds}}$

30 inches = 2 feet 6 inches = 2.5 feet

Velocity = $\dfrac{2.5 \text{ feet}}{0.2 \text{ seconds}}$

Velocity = 12.5 feet/second

Power = 1/2 x mass x velocity x velocity

P = 0.5 x 145 pounds x 12.5 x 12.5

Power = 11,328.125 foot pounds

Foreign Automotive Service, page 16

How many jobs listed should I schedule tomorrow?

Donna can schedule them all. A possible schedule is listed below; however, there are many possible alternatives to this arrangement.

TIME	HOIST I MECHANIC I	HOIST II MECHANIC II	MECHANIC III
8-9	'84 Nissan	'91 Honda Civic	'85 Audi
9-10	'84 Nissan		'85 Audi
10-11	'84 Nissan	'88 Nissan	'85 Audi
11-12	'84 Nissan		'85 Audi
12-1	LUNCH	LUNCH	LUNCH
1-2	'85 Audi	'90 Mercedes	'84 Nissan
2-3	'85 Audi		'84 Nissan
3-4	'85 Audi	'91 Golf	'84 Nissan
4-5	'85 Audi	'91 Golf	'84 Nissan

Marathon Travel, page 18

What will the price be for each person going on this tour?

$2,779 initial cost x 11% = $305.69

$2,779.00 initial cost
  306.00 agent booking fee
+ 36.00 international taxes
$3,121.00 price per person without discount

36 people booked ÷ 30 = one free trip

$3,121 cost of one trip ÷ 36 people = $86.69 savings per person

$3,121.00 price per person
  - 86.69 savings per person
$3,034.31 price after discount

> The cost will be $3,034.31 per person.

Roehl Transport, page 19

- The U.S. Department of Transportation regulations prohibit a driver from driving more than 70 hours in any 8-day period. Over the past 7 days, Mark has accumulated 54³/4 hours of driving. **Knowing this, does he have enough hours available to deliver the freight today?**

$$
\begin{array}{ll}
70 & \text{hours maximum in 8 days} \\
- 54^{3}/4 & \text{Mark has driven} \\
\hline
15^{1}/4 & \text{hours left to drive April 1st}
\end{array}
$$

510 miles x 110% = 561 miles

561 miles ÷ 50 mph = 11.22 hours to Porter, Indiana

> Yes, he does have enough hours

- **To the nearest quarter hour, what is the earliest that Mark will arrive in Porter?**

We have determined it will take 11.22 total hours of driving to get to Porter.

So far Mark has driven:

$$
\begin{array}{lll}
\text{8:15 to 1:00 pm (or 8:15 to 13:00)} \quad \text{and} & \text{1:30 to 6:30 pm} \\
\quad 13 \;\; \text{hours} & \quad 6^{1}/2 \;\; \text{hours} \\
\underline{- 8^{1}/4 \;\; \text{hours}} & \underline{- 1^{1}/2 \;\; \text{hours}} \\
\quad 4^{3}/4 \;\; \text{hours} & \quad 5 \;\;\; \text{hours}
\end{array}
$$

So...

$$
\begin{array}{lll}
\quad 4^{3}/4 \;\; \text{hours} & \quad 11.22 \;\; \text{hours driving total} \\
\underline{+ 5 \;\; \text{hours}} & \underline{- 9.75 \;\; \text{hours driven}} \\
\quad 9^{3}/4 \;\; \text{hours} & \quad 1.47 \;\;\; \text{hours left to drive} \\
& \qquad\qquad \text{(about } 1^{1}/2 \text{ hours)}
\end{array}
$$

Mark has driven 9.75 hours, and in 15 minutes he is required to stop for an 8-hour rest period. Therefore, travelling as fast as he is allowed by law, the rest of his schedule will look like this:

$+ - x \sqrt{} \pi \pm \div \geq + - x \sqrt{} \pi \pm \div \geq + - x \sqrt{} \pi \pm \div \geq + - x \sqrt{} \pi \pm \div \geq + - x \sqrt{} \pi \pm$

Real Life Math Mysteries   69

Answer Key

8:15 p.m. - 4:15 a.m.	off duty
4:15 a.m. - 4:30 a.m.	truck inspection
4:30 a.m. -	driving

4:30 + 1½ hours driving time left = 6:00 a.m.

The earliest Mark can arrive in Porter is 6 a.m.

Widmare Stables, page 20

• **Mentally calculate the cost of the two miles of white fencing installed in 1989. The fence cost $7.50 a foot, and there are more than 5,000 feet in a mile.**

Any way you get the answer is fine. But here's one easy way:

5,000 feet in a mile x 2 miles = 10,000 feet total

Next multiply $7.50 x 10,000.
You know that 7 x 10,000 = 70,000
So 7.5 x 10,000 = 75,000

$75,000.00 worth of fence

Or, if you wish to be more precise:

There are 5,280 feet in a mile	10,560
x 2 miles	x 7.50
10,560 feet of fence	$79,200

• **According to the feeding schedule, how many bales of hay should the Weigels expect to order in an average month?**

total slices = 61
61 slices x 2 daily feedings = 122 slices per day
122 slices + (1 slice x 1 daily feeding) = 123 slices
123 slices ÷ 12 slices per bale = 11 bales per day
11 + (4 other bales x 2 daily feedings) = 19 bales of hay per day

19 per day x 30 days =   570 bales per month

• **How long should they expect a ton of grain to last?**

Adding this list of fractions can be a strain. Here's a suggestion.

Ignore the handful and the a.m. only feeding for now.

Cross out and count the whole cans		=	10
Circle and add up the half cans	10/2	=	5
Cross out the zero cans		=	0
Mark and add up the quarter cans	18/4	=	4 1/2
			19 1/2 cans

(19 1/2 cans x 2 feeding) + (1/4 can x 1 feeding)
+ (1 handful x 2 feedings) =
39 1/4 + 2 handfuls = total daily feeding

We can guess that two handfuls are less than or about equal to 1/4 can.

Therefore total daily feeding = 39 1/2 cans

39 1/2 cans x 4 pounds per can = 158 pounds of grain per day

2,000 pounds per ton ÷ 158 pounds = 12.65 days

> They can expect a ton of grain to last 12 or 13 days

Boson Company, page 22

• **Calculate the number of cubic yards of Redi Mix concrete needed to pour the walls and floor.**

This problem isn't so hard if we think of it in word equations. We know that:
Volume of concrete needed = volume of walls + volume of floor

And we know:
Volume = length x width x height

You could think of the four walls as one long wall, and to find the volume you would simply multiply the length times the

$+ - x \sqrt{} \pi \pm \div \geq + - x \sqrt{} \pi \pm \div \geq + - x \sqrt{} \pi \pm \div \geq + - x \sqrt{} \pi \pm \div \geq + - x \sqrt{} \pi \pm$

Real Life Math Mysteries   71

Answer Key

width times the height. But what happens at the corners? We won't need as much concrete there. How can we keep from duplicating our concrete estimate for the corners?

There is an easy way. Think of the wall diagram like this:

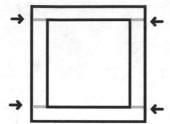

The shaded lines at the arrows show you where to "take off" the extra concrete.

You can actually cut the walls into two 24'0" walls and two 22'6" walls.

Now, we go back to our word equation: v = l x w x h
volume of walls =   2 (24'0" x 9" x 4'0") + 2 (22'6" x 9" x 4'0")

Now change inches to feet—divide by 12.
= 2 (24 x 0.75 x 4) + 2 (22.5 x 0.75 x 4)
= 2 (72) + 2 (67.5)
= 144 + 135 = 279 cubic feet

We must change the cubic feet to cubic yards.
How many feet in a cubic yard? 3 x 3 x 3 = 27
279 ÷ 27 = 10.333 cubic yards of concrete needed for the walls

Now consider the floor. Volume of floor = length x width x depth.

What is the length? The walls we know are 9" thick. Then the inside measurement of each wall must be (24'0"-9"-9") long.
Therefore, the length of each side of the floor is 22'6" long.

v = l x w x d   The depth of the floor is 6".
v = 22.5 x 22.5 x 0.5
v = 253.125 cubic feet
v = 253.125 ÷ 27 = 9.375 cubic yards

volume of walls + volume of floor = total volume of concrete

10.333 + 9.375 = 19.708 cubic yards

Contractor's estimate = 20 cubic yards of concrete

Marshfield Police Department, page 24

- **Can you show that Mr. Smith may have had a motive for setting this fire?**

Detective Jepsen imagines himself in the position of the home-owner, Mr. Smith. What could drive someone to set fire to his own house? If he was having financial difficulty, perhaps he believed the insurance money would help him to get out of debt.

    Mr. Smith makes $1,250.00 per month.
      $1,250.00 salary
       - 686.40 house payment
      $ 563.60 left

He pays $2,400.00 per year in real estate taxes.
$2,400 ÷ 12 = $200 per month
    $ 563.60
    - 200.00 real estate taxes
    $ 363.60 left

He pays $240.00 per year in house insurance.
$240 ÷ 12 = $20 per month
    $363.60
    - 20.00
    $343.60 left (It's dwindling.)

Further monthly obligations:
    $ 343.60
    - 250.00 car payments
    $ 93.60 left
    - 30.00 Master Card
    $ 63.60 left
    - 40.00 Household Finance payments
    $23.60 left
    - 120.00 boat payment
    $ - 96.40 left
    $-105.00 utilities
    $ -201.40 left

> Mr. Smith has $201.40 per month more in bills than he receives in salary. Mr. Smith had a motive. We can expect that Mr. Smith will be in jail soon.

WDLB AM, page 26

- **Now I've got to calculate if the voltage is where it's supposed to be. How do I do that?**

    I know the resistance R = 250 Ohms
    I know the current I = 0.25 amps
    I need to find the voltage E.

On the chart, the lower left quarter of the inner circle shows an E.
    This is the area I will be looking at.

Directly below the E is a formula using R and I, which I know.
    I'll choose that formula.

    E = R x I

Now plug in the numbers we know.
    E = 250 x 0.25
    E = 62.5

> The voltage should be 62.5 volts

- **Can I figure my voltage?**

We are again looking for voltage (E), so we will use the same section of the chart. However, this time we know power (P) = 50 watts, and we know resistance (R) = 1 Ohm.

Select a formula we can use.

    $E = \sqrt{P} \times R$

    $E = \sqrt{50} \times 1$

    $E = \sqrt{50}$

Your calculator can do this in a jiffy.
    E = 7.0710678

> The voltage is about 7 volts.

Wildwood Park Zoo, page 28

Change the metric quantities listed into ounces.

My dictionary lists in the index a "measures and weights table." From that I learned that 1 ounce = 31.103 grams. We can safely round that to 31 grams.

The measures given to Mr. Hlavac are listed in grams. Obviously ounces are bigger than grams, so we will have to divide.

For each gibbon food item, we will be dividing by 31. This will be a whole lot easier if we use the memory feature on the calculator:

- Push **MRC**, **M-**, **ON/C** to clear the memory.
- Push **31 M+** to add this number to the memory.
- Push **ON/C** once to return to the main keypad.
- Punch **200 divided by**
- Push **MRC** to retrieve the stored number (31)
- Push the **=** and you will see your answer.

a.m.	1/2 can Science Diet	p.m.	3 cups HiPro chow
	2 slices bread		**210 g. green beans = 7 oz.***
	1/2 c. peanuts		**210 g. celery = 7 oz.***
	1/2 c. raisins		1/2 c. sunflower seeds
	200 g. apple = 7 oz.		**270 g. orange = 10 oz.**
	90 g. banana = 3 oz.		**270 g. banana = 10 oz.**
	2 c. grapes		**143 g. sweet potato = 5 oz.**
			147 g. carrot = 5 oz.
			73 g. onion = 3 oz.
			20 g. parsley = 1 oz.
			105 g. kale = 4 oz.
			150 g. spinach = 5 oz.
			380 g. lettuce = 13 oz.

* Students who rounded 28.35 grams/ounce to 28 will get an answer of 7.5 for these items, which would correctly be rounded to **8 ounces**.

Answer Key

Ken Weis Electric, page 30

How far is it from the bottom edge of the outlet box to the floor?

The first thing to do is to write down what you know. In this case, we need to write what we know on the diagram.

$1^7/_8$"
$3^3/_4$" $4^7/_{16}$"

Now we can see what we are dealing with.

An outlet box is $3^3/_4$" tall.

$$
\begin{aligned}
\text{Half of the outlet box} \quad &= 3^3/_4 \div 2 \\
&= {}^{15}/_4 \div 2 \\
&= {}^{15}/_4 \times {}^7/_8 = {}^{15}/_8 \\
&= 1^7/_8"
\end{aligned}
$$

$4^7/_{16}$" from the drain pipe to the center of the outlet box.
$+1^7/_{16}$" from the center of the outlet box to the bottom

$$
\begin{aligned}
4^7/_{16}" \quad &= \quad 4^7/_{16}" \\
+1^7/_8" \quad &= \quad 1^{14}/_{16}" \\
\hline
5^{21}/_{16}" \quad &= \quad 6^5/_{16}" \text{ from the drain pipe to the bottom of}
\end{aligned}
$$
the outlet box

25" from the drain pipe to the floor
$-6^5/_{16}$" from the drain pipe to the bottom of the outlet box

$$
\begin{aligned}
25" \quad &= \quad 24^{16}/_{16}" \\
-6^5/_{16}" \quad &= \quad 6^5/_{16}" \\
\hline
&\quad\;\; 18^{11}/_{16}"
\end{aligned}
$$

$8^{11}/_{16}$" from bottom of outlet box to floor

Marshfield Fire and Rescue Department, page 32

- **Use the formula below to find out the minimum number of gallons per minute we're going to have to pour on that fire to put it out.**

Critical Flow = length x width ÷ 3 x # stories x % involved

Critical Flow = 50 x 100 ÷ 3 x 3 stories x 50% involved
Critical Flow = 5000 x 0.50

> Critical Flow = 2,500 gallons per minute

- **Will we have enough people to cover the fire? Or, if we have to send out for support, what is the minimum number of fire fighters we will need to request?**

30	firefighters in department	2,500	gallons needed
x 50	gallons per minute each	-1,500	covered
1,500	total gallons per minute	1,000	more gallons needed

1,000 ÷ 50 gallons per firefighter= 20 more firefighters needed

- **If you remember the critical flow you calculated, you can figure how many hoses we'll need.**

2,500 gallons per minute ÷ 250 gallons per hose per minute =
10 hoses minimum

- **Use the formula below to determine friction loss.**

Friction Loss = (2 x Q^2 + Q) x L

Q = 100 gallons per hose
Q = 250 ÷ 100 = 2.5

L = 100 feet of hose
L = 500 ÷ 100 = 5

Friction Loss = [2 x (2.5)^2 + 2.5] x 5
Friction Loss = [(2 x 6.25) + 2.5] x 5
Friction Loss = (12.5 + 2.5) x 5
Friction Loss = 15 x 5 = 75 # of friction loss

- **Find how many pounds of pressure we have to deliver from the engine, adding 5 pounds for each extra story.**

friction loss + nozzle pressure = engine pressure for 1-story
75# + 50# = 125 # engine pressure for 1-story
for 3 stories = 125 # + 5# + 5# = 135 pounds of pressure

Marshfield YMCA, page 34

- **Can we estimate that percentage from the information on this computer printout?**

Total Usage During March 1994

6 a.m.	463	12 p.m.	543	6 p.m.	1, 920
7 a.m.	559	1 p.m.	970	7 p.m.	1,263
8 a.m.	851	2 p.m.	908	8 p.m.	614
9 a.m.	683	3 p.m.	1,522	9 p.m.	192
10 a.m.	579	4 p.m.	1,467	10 p.m.	14
11 a.m.	596	5 p.m.	1,550		

The printout covers 31 days of attendance. We can average the attendance per day by adding the attendance per hour and dividing by 31.

total recorded usage in March = 14,694
14,694 ÷ 31 = 474 average attendance recorded per day

Remember that 20% of the attendees did not scan their card. Therefore, the real number of attendees is considerably larger.

474 = 80% of real total
474 = 0.80 x real total
474 ÷ 0.80 = real total
(we shifted the equation around in the same way we can shift 6 = 3 x 2 into 6 ÷ 3 = 2.)

real total = 474 ÷ 0.80 = 592.5 = an average of 593 members use it daily

There are 6,143 total members of the Marshfield YMCA. What percent use it per day?

Remember that a percentage is a part, and in this case the answer will be less than one whole. Therefore we will divide the smaller number by the bigger one.

593 ÷ 6143 = 0.0965326 = $\boxed{10\% \text{ of members use the Y each day}}$

Ask yourself. Is my answer reasonable? Does it make sense?

- **How else might Mike use these statistics?**

When is the best time for Mike to offer adult classes?

Definitely between the hours of 6 a.m. and 8 p.m., but can we be more specific? The largest attendance is from 3 p.m. until 6 or 7 p.m., but it is very possible that most of that is kids' after-school attendance. That might be a good time for kids' classes. 6 p.m. and 7 p.m. seem to be a good time, but there's a good chance that the adults who use the Y at that time just come to unwind from work and are not ready to be involved in a class then. Does it matter which classes are offered when?

Kids' classes?

It looks like 3 p.m., 4 p.m., and 5 p.m. are good times. Since most adults get off work at 5 p.m., we can guess the high attendance after that is mostly adult attendance.

When should the Y offer babysitting?

The high rate of attendance at 8 a.m., 1 p.m. and 2 p.m. is most likely from parents who do not work outside the home. Some of these people would benefit from babysitting. Are these the only hours it should be offered?

During what continuous four hours should the building supervisor be on duty?

According to attendance alone, the four busiest consecutive hours are 3 p.m., 4 p.m., 5 p.m. and 6 p.m. Are there other factors which should be considered? Why might it be good to rotate the building supervisor's schedule?

What time should the YMCA close at night?

At first it would appear the best time to close is 9:30 p.m., because so few people are using the Y at 10 p.m. However, consider that the 192 people who arrived at 9 p.m. probably plan on staying an hour or an hour and a half. Therefore, the Y should probably close at 10:30, which it does. The pools, gym and weight room close at 10:30 p.m., and the locker rooms stay open until 11 p.m. to allow people to shower and change.

What time should it open in the morning?

The YMCA opens at 5:30 a.m. according to this printout, and it seems to be widely used at that time. However, if you take those 463 attendees and divide by 31 days, you see that only 15 people are using the Y at that hour. The cost of building supervisors and lifeguards may not justify such an early opening, except as a service to members. Actually, according to Mike, no organization makes money off pools. The cost of lifeguards and upkeep plus insurance is very high.

Marshfield News-Herald, page 36

- **How much room will we have left on the page for other stories and headlines?**

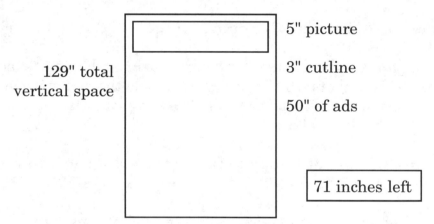

129" total vertical space

5" picture

3" cutline

50" of ads

71 inches left

- **How many inches will we have for news and what will the percentage of news to advertising be?**

```
   492  inches display ads          129  inches per page
 + 566  inches classified ads       x 20  pages
 1,058  total ad space            2,580  total space
```

```
 2,580  total space
-1,058  ad space
 1,522  news space
```

Percentage, we know, is a part of the total. Therefore, divide the smaller number by the larger—the news space divided by the total space.

News: 1522 ÷ 2580 = 0.589 = 59%
Ads: 1058 ÷ 2580 = 0.41 = 41%

$\boxed{\text{News 59\%, Ads 41\%}}$

News 59%, Ads 41%

(You know your answer makes sense if the two percentages add up to 100.)

- **What percentage of the original will achieve the required photo width?**

    We need to reduce the photo from 6⁷/₁₆ inches to 6 inches.

To find the percentage, we will divide the smaller number by the larger.
    6 ÷ 6⁷/₁₆

    To do this on a calculator, you must first change the fraction to a decimal.
    How? By dividing.

    7 ÷ 16 = 0.4375 = 0.44
    Then   6 ÷ 6.44 = 0.931677 = 93%

$\boxed{\text{93\% of the original photo}}$

City of Marshfield Engineer, page 38

- **Which is higher, the crosshair inside the level or the bench mark on which the rod is held?**

    Simplify the numbers. Looking through the level at bench mark #2, Mr. Kaczmarowski sees horizontally to about the number 5 on the level rod. Mr. Kaczmarowski must be looking from above the bottom of the rod, the spot where the bench mark is located.

- **Which is higher, bench mark #2 or bench mark #470?**

    Again, write down what you know.

Answer Key

Bench mark #2 has an elevation of 1,250.75.
Looking through the level Mr. Kaczmarowski sees 5.17 feet on the rod held on bench mark #2.

Bench mark #470 has an unknown elevation.
Looking from the same spot through his level, he sees 4.36 feet on the level rod held on bench mark #470.

Mr. Kaczmarowski has not moved. How could he see one marking at one place, and another at another place? One of the places is lower than the other. Which one?

Let's make a model. A cardboard tube can approximate for a level. A ruler is our rod. Using a model, it is easy to see that the second bench mark is higher than the first.

• **What is the elevation above sea level of bench mark #470?**

We have established that the unknown bench mark is higher than the first. How much higher? Subtract.

5.17	Therefore, the elevation of the second
-4.36	bench mark (#470) is 0.81 feet higher
0.81	than the first bench mark (#2)

1,250.75'	elevation of the first bench mark
+ .81	higher
1,261. 56	elevation of the second bench mark

The elevation of bench mark #470 is 1,261.56 feet above sea level.

Perkins Sports, page 40

• **According to the chart from the Marker© binding manufacturer, whose bindings should be set tighter?**

Jake's binding adjustment:
Step 1.   Based on Jake's weight, height, and boot length, he would need an adjustment of 6.
Step 2.   That he is a Type I skier doesn't change that. Because he is over 50, we move up the chart one code to a 5.

Ethan's binding adjustment:

Step 1.   Ethan's weight and height don't line up on the chart. His height is code L, but his weight is code J. In the interest of safety, Denny considers the lightness of his frame, and determines the release by that value (J). The release value would be 4 for his boot length.

Step 2.   However, Ethan needs a tighter binding for the aggressive skiing he does. The instructions direct you to move down the chart two codes for a type III skier. Therefore, Ethan needs a setting of 6.

> Ethan's are set tighter.

- **If a person is short and stocky, should I choose the measurement for height or for weight? Why?**

The directions instruct the adjuster to choose the one that is closer to the top of the chart, because that is the easier release value. A short person needs an easier release than a tall person, therefore height would be the deciding factor for this person.

> Height

- **Why does a person's height affect how tightly his or her bindings need to be set?**

A shorter person has less distance to fall, and so exerts less force in falling than a taller person of the same weight. That means the shorter person will need an easier binding release setting.

- **Like Brian, mentally calculate the estimate for this job.**

Find the cost of parts:	3 cables x $4 each = $12
Find the cost of labor:	15 min./cable x 4 cables = 1 hour
	1 hour @ $16 /hour = $16
Find the total cost:	$12 + $16 = $28

Now figure the tax.
     10% of $28 = $2.80
     5% of $28 = $1.40

$28 + $1.40 tax = $29.40

Brian adds a couple dollars.

> Brian will tell the customer to expect
> to pay 31 or 32 dollars.

Valley Sanitation, page 43

- **If the truck weighed in at 37,910 pounds, and weighed out at 26,090 pounds, how many tons of garbage would the truck have had on it (to the nearest 1/10 ton)?**

37,910	pounds
- 26,090	pounds
11,820	pounds

  11,820 pounds ÷ 2,000 = | 5.9 tons |

- **If the customer put six cubic yards of garbage in the dumpster weekly, and he or she is billed four times a year, how much would his or her bill be?**

  52 weeks in a year ÷ 4 = 13 weeks per billing period
  You could do this easily by dividing by 2.
  52 ÷ 2 = 26 ÷ 2 = 13

  $20 per cubic yard x 6 cubic yards = $120 per week

  $120 per week x 13 weeks in a billing period

  We know 100 x 13 = 1,300
  We know 2 x 13 = 26
  So we know 20 x 13 = 260
  1,300 + 260 = 1,560 | The bill would be $1,560.00 |

- **If a customer calls and says that he or she needs garbage picked up, and he or she lives five and a half miles from Valley Sanitation, how much would we charge?**

8 miles x 2 ways = 16 miles round trip
16 miles x 1.25 =

How are we going to do that in our heads? Easy.

16 x 1 = 16
.25 = 1/4 1/4 of 16 is 4 $16 + $4 =   ☐ $20.00

- **What do we pay a customer who brings in 43 pounds of aluminum cans, and 62 pounds of aluminum scrap material?**

  43 + 62 = 105 pounds
  105 x 0.20 = ?
  105 x 2 = 210
  105 x .2 = 21.0

  ☐ The customer would be paid $21.00.

- **How many pounds of garbage did we take in last Wednesday?** (Note to teachers: You can time your students in a race on this one. But tell them not to rush too fast. Only correct answers are accepted.)

  9,390
  12,140
  19,600
  6,420
  15,170
  690   ☐ 101,830 pounds
  14,360
  12,210
  +11,850
  101,830

- **How many tons did we take in last Wednesday (to the nearest ton)?**

  101,930 ÷ 1000 = 101.930
  Now, to divide 101.930 by 2
  100 ÷ 2 = 50 So we know it is 50 something.
  19 ÷ 2 = 9.5 So it is more than 50.9   ☐ 51 tons

Answer Key

Anthropological Studies Institute, page 46

- **Without using a calculator, find out how many centimeters he hopes its diagonal measurement will read (to the nearest centimeter).**

John knows that the length of the diagonal will be equal to the sum of the squares of its sides.

$$C^2 = a^2 + b^2$$

He knows that side a and side b are each 1 meter long because he measured them.

So: $C^2 = 1^2 + 1^2$
$$C^2 = 2$$
$$C = \sqrt{2}$$

John has the square root of two memorized. For us to find $\sqrt{2}$, we will need to do some guessing and checking. We know it will be bigger than 1, because 1 x 1 = 1. We also know it will be less than 2, because 2 x 2 = 4. Let's try some numbers in between.

$$\begin{array}{c} 1.5 \\ \underline{\times\ 1.5} \\ 2.25 \quad \text{too big} \end{array} \qquad \begin{array}{c} 1.4 \\ \underline{\times 1.4} \\ 1.96 \quad \text{almost} \end{array}$$

At this point, we might want to round our answer to 1.4 meters. But we need to find the answer to the nearest *centimeter*, which means to one more decimal place. Here's an example of how we can continue guessing and checking:

$$\begin{array}{c} 1.41 \\ \underline{\times 1.41} \\ 1.9881 \quad \text{really close!} \end{array} \qquad \begin{array}{c} 1.42 \\ \underline{\times 1.42} \\ 2.0164 \quad \text{also really close!} \end{array}$$
Which is closer?

$$\begin{array}{c} 2.0000 \\ \underline{-1.9881} \\ 0.0119 \quad \text{too small} \end{array} \qquad \begin{array}{c} 2.0164 \\ \underline{-2.0000} \\ 0.0164 \quad \text{too big} \end{array}$$
Which is closer? 1.41 meters is closer to the square root of 2.

Therefore, he is hoping the diagonal measurement will read

> **141 centimeters.**

- **Mr. Moore's question is, how many students can he hire to work 4 hours a day, 5 days a week for 10 weeks at a cost to the center of $7.50 an hour?**

$6,500	total salaries budgeted
- 3,500	Mr. Moore's salary
$3,000	student salaries

4 hours a day x 5 days a week x 10 weeks = 200 hours

200	hours
x $7.50	salary per hour for one student
$1,500	total salary one student

Therefore, $3,000 will allow for the hiring of   **two students.**

- **What is the maximum number of miles that he should plan to travel in the six-month period, based on this budget, and how many trips to the site in Marshfield would that allow?**

We have to determine first the amount budgeted for travel.
5% of 15,000 = 0.05 x 15,000 = $750 to the university for rent.

Now we can find his total expenses:

$ 750	rent, etc.
6,500	salaries
2,500	service & supplies
+3,500	miscellaneous
$13,250	except travel

$15,000	
- 13,250	
$1,750	can be budgeted for travel

Now we must find how many miles John can plan to travel.

$1,750 ÷ 0.63 per mile = 2,777.777 = **2,777 (or 2,778) miles**

2,778 miles ÷ 68 round trip miles = **about 40 trips to Marshfield**

Marshfield Clinic, page 49

- **How many mg of Amoxicillin should she receive per dose?**

    To convert pounds to kilograms, divide by 2.2

    24 pounds Kimberly's weight ÷ 2.2 = 10.9 kilograms
    10.9 kg x 40 mg Amoxicillin = 436 mg/day

    436 mg ÷ 3 doses per day = | 145 mg per dose |

- **How many ml should Kimberly receive per dose? (round to the nearest ml)**

    250 mg Amoxicillin = 5 liquid ml
    145 mg. Amoxicillin = ? ml

Kimberly's dosage (145 mg) is a percentage of the standard dosage (250 mg).

    145 ÷ 250 = 0.58 = 58% of the standard dosage

Kimberly should be given 58% of the standard liquid measure.

    58% of 5 = 5 x 0.58 = 2.9 ml or | 3 ml per dose |

- **Do we need to consider supplemental feedings?**

Joey's birth weight was 6 pounds 12 ounces
16 ounces = 1 pound

    6 # x 16 oz. = 96 ounces
    96 ounces + 12 ounces = 108 ounces

    10% of 108 = 10.8 ounces Joey could safely lose

    6 pounds 12 ounces birthweight
    6 pounds 4 ounces present weight
    8 ounces lost

    | We do not need to begin supplemental feedings. |

Aviation Services, page 50

- **How fast will we travel, and how long will it take us to fly the 150 statute miles to Minneapolis?**

$$
\begin{array}{ll}
100 & \text{knots/hour normal speed} \\
\underline{+\,10} & \text{tailwind speed} \\
110 & \text{knots/hour actual speed}
\end{array}
$$

150 statute miles to Minneapolis divided by 1.15 = 130.4 nautical miles

> The plane will be travelling at
> 110 nautical miles (knots) per hour.

150 divided by 110 = 1.36 hours

0.36 hours = 36/100 hour = how many minutes?
We know that we are looking for a part of 60.
0.36 x 60 = 21.6 minutes

> One hour and 22 minutes

For those students acquainted with algebra:

How do we know that nautical miles = statute miles divided by 1.15?

Let "n" stand for nautical miles, "s" for statute miles.

We know that nautical miles are 15% longer than statute miles.
$$s = n + .15n$$

We can combine terms to read:
$$s = 1.15\,n$$

We can divide both sides of the equation by 1.15
$$s/1.15 = n$$

Answer Key

Answer Key

- **The question is, can this plane carry this weight to Minneapolis? I'll need a complete report.**

1650	empty weight	1.36	hours in flight
172	pounds passenger	x 9	gallons per hour
218	passenger	12.24	gallons needed
136	passenger		
202	passenger	0.75	hours reserve
+190	baggage	x 9	gallons per hour
2,568	pounds	6.75	gallons needed

total gallons needed:
12.24
+ 6.75
18.99 gallons

18.99 gallons
x 6 pounds per gallon
113.94 pounds fuel

2,568 loaded weight
+114 pounds fuel
2682 pounds fully loaded

Maximum weight: 2650 pounds

No, this plane is overloaded!

As the pilot, now explain to the passengers exactly why some of them or some of their baggage cannot go. Explain the options they have.

2682 Present weight
- 2650 Maximum weight
32 pounds must be left

Out of 190 pounds baggage, something weighing at least 32 pounds must be left, or sent on another plane.

Marshfield Mayor, page 52

Do you think your students could help me come up with some convincing visuals to show the committee why we need to cut costs, particularly city employee salaries?

90 Real Life Math Mysteries

There is a lot of variation possible in how you wish to convey these statistics. On a Macintosh®, it is relatively easy to create graphics which the Mayor could use.

- **Statistics show that the biggest chunk of our city government budget (62%) goes for the salary and fringe benefits of our city employees.**

Using ClarisWorks®, a program available on most Macintosh computers, you follow these steps (if you are using an IBM with Windows, the steps are similar, but you may need to consult the User's Guide):

Click on <u>File</u>, Drag down to <u>New File</u>
Click on <u>SS</u> to create a Spreadsheet
Enter the following information as is:

	A	B	C	D
1	salary and fringe benefits		0.62	
2	other		0.38	
3				

Now click on <u>Chart</u>, drag to <u>New Pie Chart</u>.
Move the instruction window out of the way by clicking on its upper border and dragging it down.
Type in this information:

Chart Title:	Marshfield City Government Budget
Plot Values in Column:	C
From Row:	1
Through Row:	2
Column of Value Titles:	A

Now, <u>Plot It!</u> and <u>print</u>.

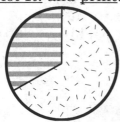

Marshfield City Government Budget

62.0% salary and fringe benefits

38.0% other

Follow the same process to create the following graphics:

- **Research has also shown that in Marshfield we are presently paying our city employees 30%-40% more than people who do similar jobs in private business.**

Answer Key

	A	B	C	D
1	Marshfield City Employee Salary			1.4
2	Comparable Private Sector Salary			1
3				

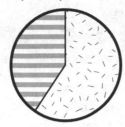

Salary Comparison

58.3% [ ] salary and fringe benefits

41.7% [ ] other

- ... **a person who owns property in Marshfield paid $1,1.68 for every $1,000 worth of property he or she owned. Compared to other cities, that's high.**

Design your spreadsheet like this:

	A	B	C	D
1	Marshfield			11.68
2	Stevens Point			9.72
3	Wausau			8.76
4	average (excluding Milwaukee)			8.77

Now click on <u>Chart</u>, drag to <u>New Series Chart</u>, and select <u>Bar Graph</u>.

Values to be Plotted: Vertical Scale:
1st Row: <u>1</u>   <u>numeric</u>
2nd Row: <u>2</u>
3rd Row: <u>3</u>
4th Row: <u>4</u>   Chart Title: <u>Property Tax Comparison</u>
From Column: <u>D</u>   Vertical Scale Title: (blank)
To Column: <u>D</u>   Horiz Scale Title: <u>$ paid per 1,000 value</u>
    Data Legends in Column: <u>A</u>
    Horizontal Titles in Row: (blank)

Now <u>Plot It!</u> and <u>Print</u>:

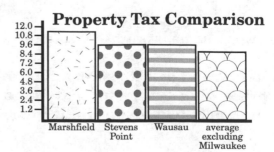

Property Tax Comparison

Answer Key

Prufrock Press, page 55

- **If the names can be in any order, how many possible combinations are there?**

Problem Solving Strategy:
Make a list of possiblities, and work systematically.

Making a list of possibilities can be kind of like weeding a garden—you think you've got them all, and turn around only to find a whole new batch of weeds you'd forgotten.

The trick, at least in math, where numbers usually don't keep growing when your back is turned, is to work systematically. Have a plan of organization and follow through with it.

Of course, you may wish to try to solve this problem without a plan of organization and that's fine. We'll keep track of who finishes first.

Systematically thinking, I'm going to break this down. There are four choices for the first position: either Carmen, Carrie, Esther, or David. So I'm going to start by writing down all the possibilities if I mention Carmen, the oldest child, first.

Carmen, Carrie, Esther, David
Carmen, Carrie, David, Esther

Carmen, Esther, Carrie, David
Carmen, Esther, David, Carrie

Carmen, David, Carrie, Esther
Carmen, David, Esther, Carrie

I found a total of 6 possibilities starting with Carmen.

Now let's think of the possibilities using Carrie first.
It will be basically the same. There will be 6 possibilities.

Now Esther first.
6 possibilities.

Answer Key

Now David first.
6 possibilities.

So the total number of possibilities is
6 + 6 + 6 + 6

$$\boxed{24 \text{ possibilities}}$$

Another way to do this problem is by multiplying the number of possibilities for each of the four positions together.

There are four possibilities for each position, right?
Wrong.

There are four possibilities for the first position.

There are only three possibilities for the next position.

Likewise, there are only two for the next position.

And there will only be one possibility left by the time you get to the last space.

Therefore, to find the total number of possibilities, we have to multiply

4 x 3 x 2 x 1, and we get 24.

Answer Key

About the Author

Mary Ford Washington has a masters degree in gifted and talented education from the University of Wisconsin and has taught gifted and talented students since 1988.

"Many times the students I teach are smarter than I am. I enjoy their brilliance. I also enjoy bringing out gifts in children whose talents and gifts are less readily accessible."

She is a single parent of four children. The oldest attends Harvard University.

In her free time Mary likes to train for cross-country ski races and triathlons, where she often finishes last. The Washington family does not own a television.